I0039103

Digital Government in Lebanon

GOVERNANCE FOR COHERENT AND SUSTAINABLE POLICY IMPLEMENTATION

OECD

BETTER POLICIES FOR BETTER LIVES

This document, as well as any data and map included herein, are without prejudice to the status of or sovereignty over any territory, to the delimitation of international frontiers and boundaries and to the name of any territory, city or area.

The statistical data for Israel are supplied by and under the responsibility of the relevant Israeli authorities. The use of such data by the OECD is without prejudice to the status of the Golan Heights, East Jerusalem and Israeli settlements in the West Bank under the terms of international law.

Note by Turkey
The information in this document with reference to "Cyprus" relates to the southern part of the Island. There is no single authority representing both Turkish and Greek Cypriot people on the Island. Turkey recognises the Turkish Republic of Northern Cyprus (TRNC). Until a lasting and equitable solution is found within the context of the United Nations, Turkey shall preserve its position concerning the "Cyprus issue".

Note by all the European Union Member States of the OECD and the European Union
The Republic of Cyprus is recognised by all members of the United Nations with the exception of Turkey. The information in this document relates to the area under the effective control of the Government of the Republic of Cyprus.

Please cite this publication as:
OECD (2020), *Digital Government in Lebanon: Governance for Coherent and Sustainable Policy Implementation*, OECD Digital Government Studies, OECD Publishing, Paris, *https://doi.org/10.1787/a711b0c1-en*.

ISBN 978-92-64-55152-7 (print)
ISBN 978-92-64-84533-6 (pdf)

OECD Digital Government Studies
ISSN 2413-1954 (print)
ISSN 2413-1962 (online)

Foreword

Rapid developments in digital technologies, data and their applications present opportunities and challenges for governments in their quest and journey to deliver greater value to citizens and businesses. In light of the COVID-19 pandemic, it is now more important than ever for governments to accelerate their digital transformation to demonstrate the resilience and agility that societies and economies expects from public sector organisations.

The Government of Lebanon recognises the potential of "going and being digital". In particular, the Office of the Minister of State for Administrative Reform (OMSAR) has been supporting ministries to drive the digital transformation by developing new public services and laying the foundations of enablers such as interoperability and digital identity frameworks. The design of the Lebanon Digital Transformation: Strategies to Action (2020-2030) Volume 1 (referred to in this report as the digital transformation draft strategy), and the Lebanon Digital Transformation (2020-2030): Implementation Plan Volume 2 (referred to in this report as its action plan), reflect the government's commitment to a sound digital government policy as a critical enabler for improved social well-being and sustainable economic development. At the same time, there is much room for improvement in terms of leadership and co-ordination for the digital transformation.

This OECD Digital Government Study of Lebanon assesses the main elements of the governance of digital government and provides action-oriented policy recommendations to help the Government of Lebanon improve the efficiency, efficacy, coherence and sustainability of its digital government policy and process.

This study was prepared at the request of OMSAR of Government of Lebanon. It refers to and builds upon the analytical framework provided by the OECD Recommendation of the Council on Digital Government Strategies, adapts the E-Leaders Handbook on Governance and leverages the OECD's expertise on digital government developed through similar projects since 2001. The study brought together experts and policy practitioners from several countries to provide peer insights for a comprehensive approach. The OECD Digital Government survey 1.0 was also undertaken by OMSAR, whose insights have informed this study.

Acknowledgements

Within the framework of the MENA-OECD Programme, the Digital Government Study of Lebanon was prepared by the Directorate for Public Governance (GOV) of the OECD, under the leadership of Acting Director, Janos Bertok.

The study was produced by GOV's Open and Innovative Government Division (OIG), under the supervision of Barbara-Chiara Ubaldi, Deputy Head of Division and Head of the Digital Government and Data Unit in OIG.

The introduction, chapters 1 and 2 were drafted by Zina Akrout and Ethel Hui Yan Tan, Junior Policy Researchers and Advisors in GOV/OIG. Chapter 3 was drafted by Ethel Hui Yan Tan. All chapters benefited from the strategic direction and revisions of Barbara-Chiara Ubaldi and João Ricardo Vasconcelos, Digital Government Policy Analyst in GOV/OIG. João Ricardo Vasconcelos also served as the lead co-ordinator for the Digital Government Study. Alison Rygh, former Digital Government Secondee, supported the initial management of the project. Karine Badr, Open Government Policy Analyst in GOV/OIG, reviewed and provided comments. Liz Zachary edited and prepared the document for publication and Liv Gaunt provided administrative support.

The OECD Working Party of Senior Digital Government Officials (E-Leaders) provided the essential knowledge and background for the development of the current review. The E-Leaders come from OECD member and non-member countries and develop digital government policy guidance with the OECD on how governments can maximise the potential and fulfil the principal functions of digital technologies and data in innovative, open, transparent, sustainable and resilient ways. The OECD is especially grateful to the following national peer reviewers from Italy and Portugal who provided valuable direction and contributions to the review:

- Giulia Temperini, International Activities Co-ordination Officer at the Agency for Digital Italy (AgID), Presidency of the Council of Ministers, Italy;
- Pedro Viana, Director of Digital Transformation, Agency for Administrative Modernisation, Ministry of State Modernisation and Public Administration, Portugal.

This project would not have been possible without the support of the Office of the Minister of State for Administrative Reform (OMSAR) of Lebanon, and benefited greatly from the assistance of Nasser Israoui, Director of the Technical Co-operation Unit at OMSAR, as well as May Baaklini and Joe Hage, former advisors at OMSAR. The review team wishes to acknowledge the important contributions provided by the many stakeholders from the public and private sector during the fact-finding interviews during the mission to Beirut in June 2019. Finally, the OECD wishes to thank the Italian Ministry of Foreign Affairs and International Co-operation and the Italian Agency for Development Co-operation for the support they have provided throughout the project.

Table of contents

Boxes

Follow OECD Publications on:

http://twitter.com/OECD_Pubs

http://www.facebook.com/OECDPublications

http://www.linkedin.com/groups/OECD-Publications-4645871

http://www.youtube.com/oecdilibrary

http://www.oecd.org/oecddirect/

Executive summary

Technological advances provide a path to unlocking greater and more sustainable economic growth and development. At the same time, they have a profound impact on society – affecting the way people interact, transact and relate to each other and devices. Governments have a responsibility to strategically manage the innovation, deployment and use of digital technologies and data with systemic thinking and agile approaches. They must consider the range and depth of policy interventions required, and the new approaches needed to design and deliver public policies and services in the digital age in ways that fit the changing expectations of citizens and businesses. This is fundamental where governments need to prove their resilience and agility while responding to critical situations such as the COVID-19 pandemic.

The Government of Lebanon understands the value of digital government as a way to champion a more efficient, innovative, open, transparent, inclusive, engaging and sustainable public sector that delivers greater value through its policies and services. This was demonstrated by its long experience in strategising the transition from e-government to digital government, strong political will to commit to the digital transformation of the public sector and a broad national consensus on the merits of digital government. The Government of Lebanon also acknowledges the need to develop new ways to interact with its citizens and businesses and build economic and social value through improved digital collaboration in its move towards digital government.

The Government of Lebanon's current digital transformation draft strategy and action plan – the *Lebanon Digital Transformation: Strategies to Action (2020-2030) Volume 1* – illustrates the government's dedication to the digital development of the country and involves the administration, private sector and civil society stakeholders. However, given the political, economic and social instability, chronic problems of siloed and uncoordinated policy efforts, as well as different levels of digital maturity across the administration, several previous transformation attempts have not been successful and originated some observable reform fatigue in the country. Therefore, securing an effective implementation of this digital transformation draft strategy is a critical challenge for the Government of Lebanon. Achieving a successful digital transformation of the government and public sector requires institutional cohesion and horizontal co-operation. The transformation is also dependent on other critical variables such as permanent political support, a clear and solid institutional mandate, key co-ordination mechanisms and strategic policy levers. Strong leadership will ensure that the action plan is carefully co-ordinated and strategically integrated across policy agendas and public sector organisations. A reinforced governance structure will ensure the effective execution of the policies across the public sector. Strengthening the leadership and mandate of the Office of the Minister of State of Administrative Reform (OMSAR) in the execution and co-ordination of the digital transformation action plan will be another positive step in this direction.

The Government of Lebanon's ability to use digital technologies to modernise its public sector and facilitate a more homogenous and sustainable distribution of development across the public administration requires the institutional capacity and policy levers to identify, prepare, co-ordinate and track information and communication technology (ICT) investments. With a better understanding of the needs of its citizens, businesses and public servants, the Government of Lebanon will be in a better position to adopt and implement a strategic approach that defines common standards and embeds a user and data-driven culture throughout the public sector.

Key policy recommendations

Strengthen public sector leadership and co-ordination

- Strengthen OMSAR's role in charge of executing the digital transformation draft strategy and supervising Digital Transformation Units (DTUs) across the administration, by clarifying its leadership, responsibilities and co-ordinating role of digital government policies.
- Explore the creation of a new public sector organisation under OMSAR with an operational mandate to digitally transform the public sector, such as the Lebanese Digital Agency foreseen in the digital transformation draft strategy, if alternatives, such as reinforcing the mandate and capacities of OMSAR, are considered insufficient.
- Consider establishing a lead function like a national chief information officer at OMSAR with an official mandate to secure strong oversight and accountability of decisions.
- Explore the creation of chief data officers and chief security officers in OMSAR and other public sector organisations to ensure the smooth adoption of digital government initiatives across the public sector, and co-ordinate and enforce data and cyber security policies.

Institutionalise collaboration within the digital government ecosystem

- Encourage greater involvement from the ecosystem of digital government stakeholders within the public sector for better policy alignment and value creation through coherent and sustainable policy implementation, shared ownership and responsibility in the development of a digitally enabled state.
- Reinforce user-driven thinking, innovation and awareness of new technological developments so the digital government ecosystem in the public sector can respond proactively to critical problems and deliver public value according to the resources available, even in critical moments, such as the COVID-19 pandemic.
- Consider increasing involvement, accountability and transparency by strengthening close collaborations between the public sector and the private sector, civil society and citizens to explore how technologies can be well-managed by public sector organisations and used in a timely and trustworthy manner.
- Develop a system of open consultation and feedback with other public sector, private sector and civil society organisations, in support of the legislative branch of the government such that digital laws and regulations can be enacted efficiently and with consideration of various stakeholders involved.

Establish policy levers to support the digital transformation implementation

- Establish standardised policy levers across the public sector under OMSAR's leadership, such as common business case methodologies for ICT procurement and commissioning, budget thresholds and pre-evaluation of ICT investments to improve the coherence and sustainability of policy implementation.
- Reinforce institutional structures, frameworks and approaches for the improved management of digital government projects, such as data capture, risk management and monitoring incentives for better implementation, evaluation and measurement of project performance.

- Build normative mechanisms and a culture of early sharing of practices, testing and feedback of digital government projects so stakeholders in the public sector are better aligned on the on-going digital transformation initiatives from policy design to implementation.

Continue to establish and update effective general and sector-specific legal and regulatory frameworks, such as the commissioning of digital technologies, while enhancing the digital transformation of the public sector in an agile way that enables a collaborative and experimental culture across the administration that goes beyond legalistic approaches.

Chapter 1. Introduction: Strengthening the governance of digital government

In recent years, governments have undertaken large-scale public sector changes to modernise their operating processes, policies and programmes and adapt to new technologies and demands from the public. Digitalisation has become a top priority for many governments and public administrations to achieve outcomes such as the digitalisation of public services, the opening up of public sector data or the establishment of common platforms shared by various public authorities to foster horizontal integration and synergies. Public sector digital transformation is a complex process that revamps both citizens' access to information and services, and the transparency and efficiency of the functioning and structure of public institutions. On the one hand, it is about assisting people through innovative and agile continuous improvement in a streamlined, straightforward and co-constructed partnership with different stakeholders. On the other hand, it is about allowing civil servants to respond to a changing organisation while maintaining the continuity of approaches, daily supervision and assessment, and introducing innovative activities (OECD, 2014[1]).

Majority of countries have made significant progress in digitalising government structures and facilities by transferring to the digital world what was previously paper-based (see Figure 1.1 on the differentiation between e-government and digital government). Becoming a fully digital government involves government-wide co-ordination to foster coherent use of digital technologies across policy areas and all levels of government, and the alignment of actions and practices within and between public sector organisations in line with broad government strategic objectives. Doing so ensures that citizens and businesses can foster partnerships with ease to co-create public policies and programmes to improve economic productivity and social well-being. Governance structures are essential to maintain active management and co-ordination and promote system-based rather than silo-driven decisions. With stronger leadership, co-ordination and collaboration, policy makers can accelerate the digital transformation of the public sector more efficiently, effectively and ensure the stability needed to deliver long-term sustainable outcomes. The most prevalent problems and obstacles are related to legacy-driven organisational structures mainly defined by vertical hierarchical institutional arrangements and silos that hamper the transition toward more consistent capital and programming cycles. Nevertheless, countries are progressively emphasising horizontal integration-oriented behaviour. This is required to promote the use of digital technologies to facilitate links between strategic policy initiatives across different sectors and government levels and to maintain policy coherence and long-term stability. Institutional set-ups need to be re-evaluated and adapted to assist a whole-of-government transition, which delivers better outcomes and helps meet the increasing demands of people (OECD, forthcoming[2]).

Figure 1.1. Digital transformation of the public sector

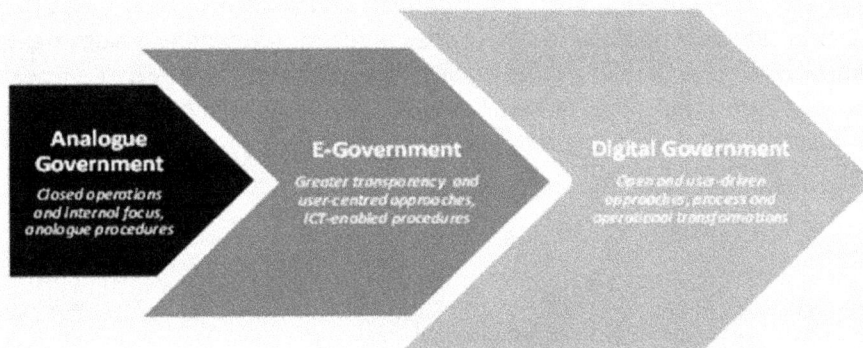

Source: Based on (OECD, 2014[1]), Recommendation of the Council on Digital Government Strategies, www.oecd.org/gov/digital-government/Recommendation-digitalgovernment-strategies.pdf.

Governance structures that maintain active co-ordinated management and promote system-based rather than silo-driven decisions are vital for policy makers to be able to evaluate and experiment with systems and technologies that are digital by design and open by default. This approach maintains the use of digital tools and information in ways that prevent amplifying existing or creating new bias. Data and digital technology management in public sector organisations also need to respond to the significant changes in our digital era and help overcome siloed policy approaches (OECD, forthcoming[2]).

Based on the OECD's experience of global policy assessments, the research of the E-Leaders Task Force on Governance and the 2014 OECD Recommendation on Digital Government Strategies (OECD, 2014[1]) (see Box 1.1 and Figure 1.2) the E-Leaders Handbook on Governance has defined three facets of governance for the digital transformation of governments that are generally applicable to all countries: contextual factors; institutional models; and policy levers (see Figure 1.3).

- Contextual factors provide an understanding of country-specific and region-specific elements and identify issues to be included in the consideration, design and implementation of policies.
- Institutional models illustrate the various forms of governance, institutional frameworks and regulatory systems in countries and how they affect and drive modern governance approaches.
- Policy levers are instruments of a democratic governance system defined by the OECD as crucial elements for strong governance to achieve a successful digital transition of the public sector.

12 |

Box 1.1. OECD Recommendation of the Council on Digital Government Strategies

Adopted on 15 July 2014, the OECD Recommendation is a structuring element for decision-makers and stakeholders that need to navigate government objectives and resources in an increasingly complex policymaking environment.

Digital technologies create both opportunities and challenges for successful government reforms in any policy domain, such as welfare, economic development, administrative services efficiency. A set of 12 key recommendations – grouped under three pillars on "openness and engagement", "governance and co-ordination", "capacities to support implementation" – are designed to guide decision-makers.

Figure 1.2. OECD Recommendation of the Council on Digital Government Strategies

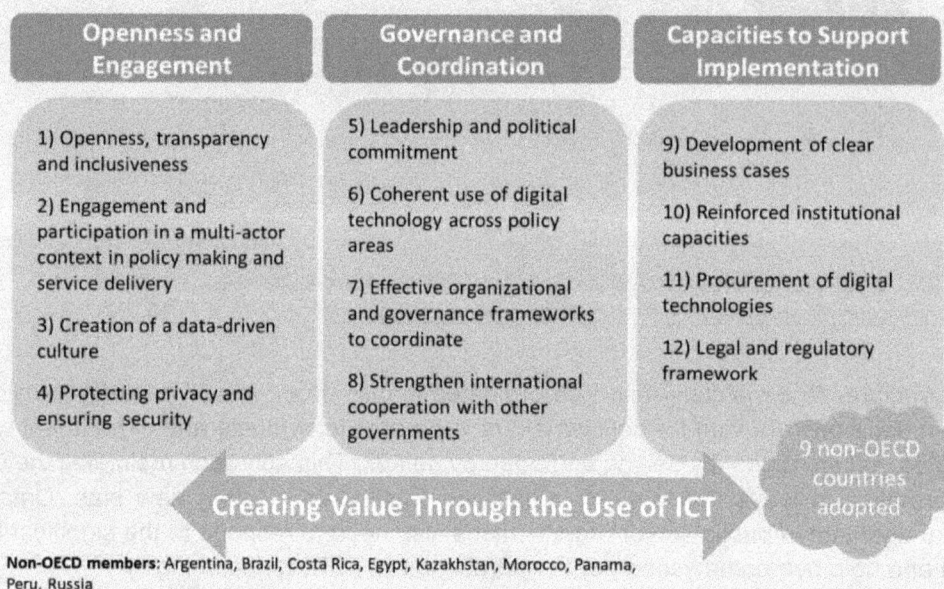

Openness and Engagement	Governance and Coordination	Capacities to Support Implementation
1) Openness, transparency and inclusiveness	5) Leadership and political commitment	9) Development of clear business cases
2) Engagement and participation in a multi-actor context in policy making and service delivery	6) Coherent use of digital technology across policy areas	10) Reinforced institutional capacities
3) Creation of a data-driven culture	7) Effective organizational and governance frameworks to coordinate	11) Procurement of digital technologies
4) Protecting privacy and ensuring security	8) Strengthen international cooperation with other governments	12) Legal and regulatory framework

9 non-OECD countries adopted

Creating Value Through the Use of ICT

Non-OECD members: Argentina, Brazil, Costa Rica, Egypt, Kazakhstan, Morocco, Panama, Peru, Russia

Source: (OECD, 2014[1]), Recommendation of the Council on Digital Government Strategies, www.oecd.org/gov/digital-government/Recommendation-digitalgovernment-strategies.pdf.

Figure 1.3. Three facets of governance for digital governments

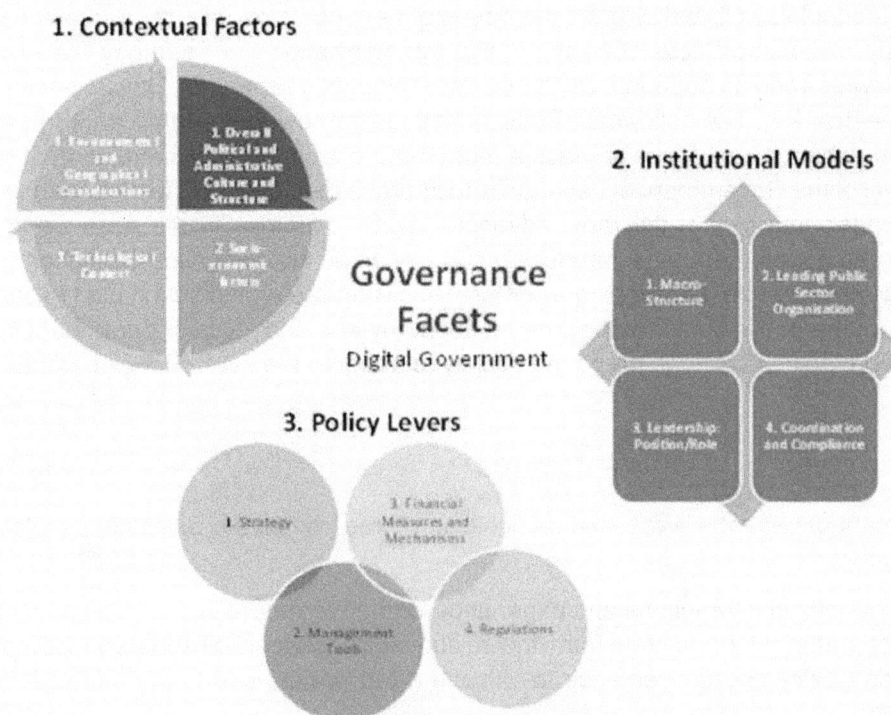

Source: (OECD, forthcoming[2]), OECD E-Leaders Governance Handbook.

For many years, Lebanon's administration has suffered from inadequate service delivery, operational inefficiencies, outdated technology, time-consuming procedures, corruption issues and dysfunctional governance systems (World Bank, 2016[3]). These problems have slowly weakened public confidence in the government, damaged Lebanon's public sector and hindered its ability to cope with the rapid pace of technological transition of the digital age. The divide continues to grow between citizens' aspirations, particularly the digital-savvy youth of today, and the outdated structures underlying many public services' existing provision (OMSAR, 2019[4]). With the civil protests in Lebanon beginning in October 2019 against the government, the need for the public sector to deliver greater value to citizens and businesses is greater than ever. Lebanon pledged, at the Paris CEDRE conference in April 2018, to conduct structural and budgetary reforms to benefit from the release of USD 11.5 billion of loans and donations promised at this conference. These investments should finance the first of the three phases of the national infrastructure rehabilitation and modernisation plan of the country, including digital transformation. However, the difficulty of the Government of Lebanon to implement strategic reforms has led the donors to withhold these loans and donations.

Successive governments have repeatedly recognised the importance of technology as a crucial way to promote innovation, reform public management, and transform public service delivery. Considerable public resources have been spent on projects to continue improving the status quo. However, judging by the expectations and experiences of users, the current situation is still unsatisfactory. In June 2019, the OECD undertook a fact-finding mission to Beirut for discussions with several senior executives in both the public and private sectors to gain insights into Lebanon's digital government needs and public perception of current government services and performance. The Lebanese stakeholders agreed that excessive focus has been put on implementing software and programmes, while the policy goal must be to digitalise state processes and services to better respond to Lebanon's population aspirations and needs.

The goal of digital transformation should not be to introduce new and complex software and programmes. The goal of establishing a digital government is to simplify government processes by integrating current and emerging technologies to better meet the needs of Lebanon's people, residents and visitors. In 2018, the Government of Lebanon developed the digital transformation draft strategy that includes an action plan, as well as wide-ranging support from investors in the public sector, the private sector and the citizens of Lebanon (see Box 1.2). The policy calls for an ambitious framework to significantly improve public digital services so that Lebanon can aspire to reach a more mature technological development status. From now to 2030, the goal of the Government of Lebanon is to improve the quality of life of its people and businesses by turning Lebanon into one of the most advanced digital countries in the Arab world, by maintaining effective and open government, and introducing citizen-centric digital services to better serve inhabitants, tourists and business people. Developing a comprehensive strategy and action plan to carry out the digital transformation of the public sector alongside the economy and society is of paramount importance – and this strategy and plan must include preparing society to adapt to the ever-changing trends of digitalisation.

Box 1.2. Main objectives of the Government of Lebanon's digital transformation draft strategy

The Government of Lebanon is focused on achieving three immediate objectives and outcomes within the first five years:

1. Improve citizen interactions and experience with government services by providing end to end services efficiently and transform the relationship between citizens and government making service quality and convenience to citizens a top priority and being more responsive to their needs.

2. Enable Lebanon's digital economy and private sector to prosper in the co-development of the emerging national and regional digital economies and to progressively form a substantial part of the government's digital supply chain. By streamlining procurement processes, we aim to make it easier for local entrepreneurs, small and medium enterprises (SME), and startups, to compete fairly and win government projects.

3. Transform public sector operations by embracing digital technology, driving for paperless processes, enabling digital by design operations based on international standards, and building a framework that delivers transformation across the entire government.

Source: (OMSAR, 2019[4]), Lebanon Digital Transformation: Strategies to Actions (2020 – 2030).

The next three chapters of this study detail and discuss the digital transformation draft strategy of Lebanon based on each of the facets identified in the E-Leaders Handbook on Governance, its dimensions and sub-dimensions and see how they can be applied to and improve the current governance framework.

From the OECD fact-finding mission to Beirut in June 2019, the strengths of the Government of Lebanon were found to include: 1) long experience in developing digital government policies; 2) a strong political will to improve and change; and 3) existing digital capacities in public and private sectors. In contrast, the discovered weaknesses were: 1) political instability; 2) public administration systems operating in silos; 3) fatigue from a history of unsuccessful digital government reform attempts; 4) low levels of digitalisation throughout the public sector; and 5) a critical public perception on corruption.

> **Box 1.3. Preliminary observations from OECD fact-finding mission, June 2019**
>
> - Ensure continuity with the 2018 Lebanon Digital Transformation: Strategies to Action (2020-2030) Volume 1.
> - Establish a balance between developing the basis, but also an ambition of "leapfrogging".
> - Leverage the positive momentum among the various stakeholders.
> - Adopt a whole-of-government approach to the strategy and implementation plan development.
> - Collaborate for shared responsibility even if this means reducing the level of ambition of the implementation plan.
> - Collect inputs, raising awareness and developing co-design sessions.
> - Prioritise involving all sectors of government, different levels of government, academia, the private sector, non-governmental organisations, and civil society.
> - Communicate that digital transformation is not a technical process.
> - Reform laws and regulations to enable better procedures, accountability, and performance monitoring.
> - Re-consider budgets strategically (investment and savings).
> - Highlight drivers for digital transformation, such as efficiency in the public sector, economic productivity, trust in government and wellbeing.
> - Attribute measures of the action plan to ministries and public administrations and prepare ministerial action plans.
> - Monitor and evaluate for accountability and Improve and communicate continuously.

Informed by the OECD's Secretariat of a Handbook on Governance for Digital Government and the outcomes of the fact-finding mission to Beirut in June 2019 (see Box 1.3), this study aims to provide guidance on sound governance tools for digital government in Lebanon based on the Lebanon Digital Transformation: Strategies to Action (2020-2030) Volume 1 (OMSAR, 2019[4]). The study highlights the contextual factors, institutional models and policy levers that could be taken into consideration when identifying the adequate elements needed to ensure the sound implementation of digital transformation in Lebanon.

References

OECD (2014), *Recommendation of the Council on Digital Government Strategies*, https://legalinstruments.oecd.org/en/instruments/OECD-LEGAL-0406. [1]

OECD (forthcoming), "OECD Digital Government Project: E-Leaders Governance Handbook", *E-Leaders Task Force on Governance*. [2]

OMSAR (2019), *Lebanon Digital Transformation: Strategies to Actions (2020 – 2030)*, Office of the Minister of State for Administrative Reform, Republic of Lebanon, Beirut.. [4]

World Bank (2016), *Lebanon: Promoting Poverty Reduction and Shared Prosperity*, [3]
http://documents.worldbank.org/curated/en/951911467995104328/pdf/103201-REPLACEMNT-PUBLIC-Lebanon-SCD-Le-Borgne-and-Jacobs-2016.pdf.

Chapter 2. **Contextual factors**

Contextual analysis of factual elements is essential for finding appropriate and informed solutions in a variety of social, economic, political and cultural contexts. When establishing a strategy for digital governments, it is of paramount importance to consider the wide range of contextual factors that can affect the ability to mobilise and co-ordinate efforts across policy areas and levels of government. "[C]ontextual factors are all the elements of the environment within which some phenomenon occurs: either the micro-context of the immediate situation or the macro-context of social, cultural, historical, political, environmental, legal and/or economic circumstances and conditions, seen as relevant to the description or analysis of any phenomenon" (OECD, forthcoming[1]). Integrating adaptability with strong understanding of contextual factors will also ensure an efficient integration and organisation of resources through the public sector. It helps authorities better align with the digital transformation strategies and policies, including main enablers, guidelines and practices, as well as the related rules and regulations.

Traditional situational considerations examined by the OECD when conducting research include data on the administrative culture, that includes the institutional and organisational characteristics, of the country. These include the electoral system of the parliament, the configuration of the executive branch, the division of power between one central and local governments, and the essential features of the judicial system. Political and legal criteria help to decode the governance structure of countries, their management and organisational approach. Under the leadership of the E-Leaders Task Force, the OECD decided to include the micro-context of the circumstances surrounding the governance of digital government and the macro-context of the broad social, cultural, geographical, financial, environmental, legal and/or economic circumstances and conditions deemed to be essential to the definition or evaluation of any event (see Figure 2.1). The interlocking circle of digitalisation and economic and social changes calls for the need to incorporate considerations other than the standard policy features that are typically considered when discussing governance in modern societies and adopting emerging governance strategies (OECD, forthcoming[1]).

In the following sections, the contextual factors of the E-Leaders governance framework will be applied and adapted to Lebanon according to four dimensions: 1) overall political and administrative culture and structure; 2) socio-economic factors; 3) technological context; 4) environmental and geographical considerations – with short analyses following sub-dimensions that were selected as relevant to the topic of digital government governance.

Figure 2.1. Digital government contextual factors

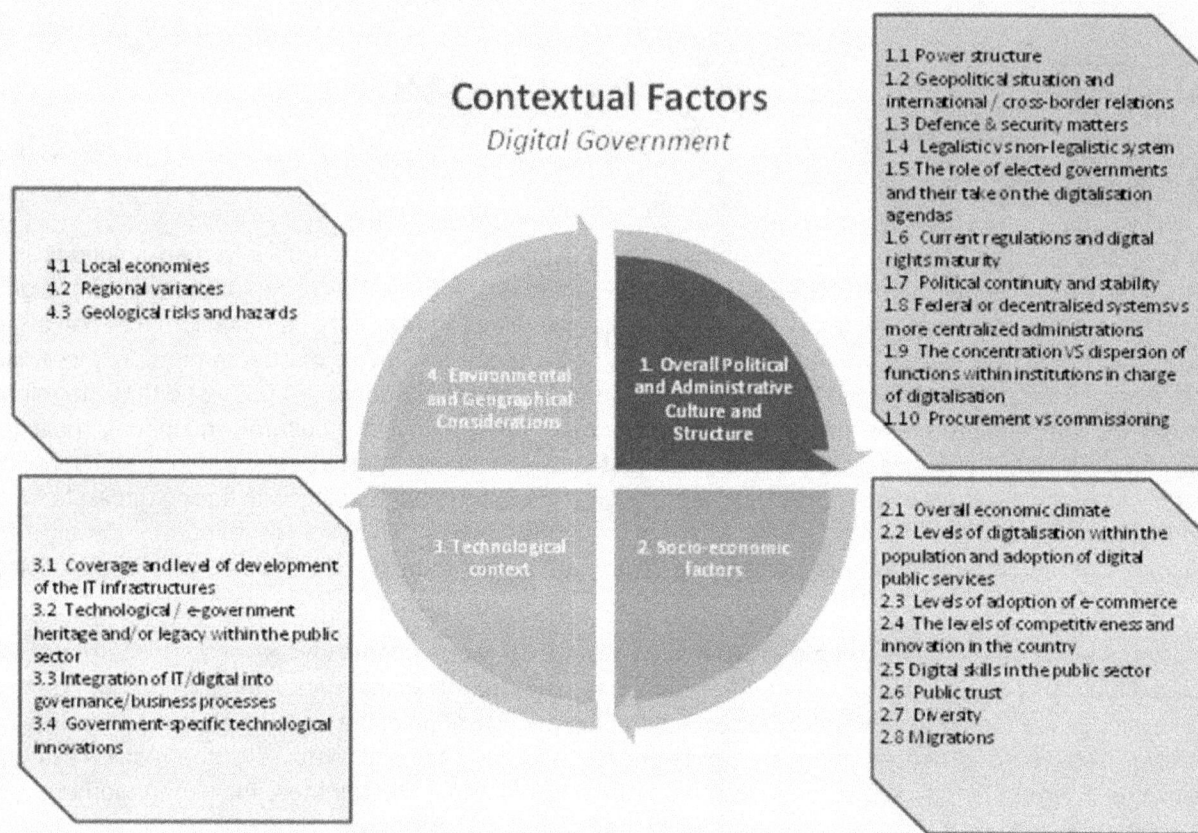

Contextual Factors
Digital Government

4.1 Local economies
4.2 Regional variances
4.3 Geological risks and hazards

1.1 Power structure
1.2 Geopolitical situation and international / cross-border relations
1.3 Defence & security matters
1.4 Legalistic vs non-legalistic system
1.5 The role of elected governments and their take on the digitalisation agendas
1.6 Current regulations and digital rights maturity
1.7 Political continuity and stability
1.8 Federal or decentralised systems vs more centralized administrations
1.9 The concentration VS dispersion of functions within institutions in charge of digitalisation
1.10 Procurement vs commissioning

3.1 Coverage and level of development of the IT infrastructures
3.2 Technological / e-government heritage and/or legacy within the public sector
3.3 Integration of IT/digital into governance/business processes
3.4 Government-specific technological innovations

2.1 Overall economic climate
2.2 Levels of digitalisation within the population and adoption of digital public services
2.3 Levels of adoption of e-commerce
2.4 The levels of competitiveness and innovation in the country
2.5 Digital skills in the public sector
2.6 Public trust
2.7 Diversity
2.8 Migrations

Source: (OECD, forthcoming[1]), OECD E-Leaders Governance Handbook.

Dimension 1. Overall political and administrative culture and structure

Referring to the E-Leaders Handbook on Governance, the "overall political and administrative culture and structure" should be understood as a dimension that considers "the administrative and institutional features of each country. These include the composition and electoral system of the legislature, the structure of the executive branch, the division of power between one central and several regional or local governments, and critical characteristics of the judicial system, but also everything about civic engagement and the political behaviour of citizens" (OECD, forthcoming[1]).

Power structure: How power is organised or shared in the country

Lebanon is a unitary state with a parliamentary political system. The partisan system is generally associated multi-party systems. The main challenge to institutional stability in Lebanon is associated with the fact that the biggest political parties in the country are confessionalist and face the historic and political legacy from the country's civil war from 1975 to 1990. This means that the coalitions necessary to form a government can be politically fragile, and their collapse leads to very regular changes in the government.

A unitary state is more likely to benefit from executive and legislative powers that can more easily and efficiently design and implement coherent digital government policies across different sectors and levels of government. This can contribute to the agility and co-ordination of the digital transformation. However, a very competitive and fragmented multi-party confessional system may pose a threat to secure coherent decisions, leadership and political commitment to the digital government strategy, as the priorities of each political party may pull decision on different directions. Given this context, the Government of Lebanon should focus on strengthening the leadership and co-ordination capacities of the public sector institution responsible for the digital government in the country, which is the Office of the Minister of State for Administrative Reform (OMSAR). The continuity of its mandate, leadership and staff beyond the different political cycles should also be considered a priority, as well as the establishing a formal position appointing someone with the official mandate and political support to act as lead of the digital transformation of the public sector, such as a Chief Information Officer (CIO) or Chief Digital Transformation Officer (CDO).

Geopolitical situation and international/ cross-border relations: All types of relationships, based on formal agreements or not, between countries

The geopolitical instability involving Lebanon in the last decades affects domestic politics and economic development, and inevitably affects Lebanon's capacity building, organisation and co-ordination of public governance strategies and plans namely around digitally transforming its government. The Government of Lebanon should strengthen efforts to ensure continuity with its digital transformation draft strategy. Effective implementation of the strategy should be considered as a public policy priority beyond the political cycle changes.

Legalistic versus non-legalistic system: The level of government support for digital government issues and current regulations and digital rights maturity

The Lebanese legal system is inspired by the French legal system, which is a civil law country. Most of the laws, decrees and rulings controlling and overseeing the operation of public sector institutions in Lebanon go back to the late 1950s and early 1960s, with small changes adopted at later stages It follows a strong principle of legality, highly codified rules of law and a centralised administrative system. Adopting legalistic or bureaucratic approaches to innovation, experimentation and commissioning may hinder the policy and co-ordination agility that is crucial for digital government development. The Government of Lebanon needs to be conscious that beyond the need of an updated legal and regulatory framework, enhancing the digital transformation of its public sector is not a static process, but requires agile, collaborative and experimental approaches across the administration.

The Government of Lebanon is aware of the importance of legal standards and compliance and agrees that standardisation will improve the quality and consistency of users' digital experience, and guarantee compliance with international norms. The plan is to create standards, guidelines and frameworks covering industry regulations and digital rights for all government agencies: cyber security, cloud security, use of personal data, digital assurance, change management. Lebanon's compliance with the privacy laws of the European Union's General Data Protection Regulation (GDPR), Lebanon's E-Transactions and Personal Data Law of October 2018, Data Privacy Law and Data Security Law are a few examples of such standards and guidelines. The Government of Lebanon is taking an active role in codifying these intentions into legislation by designing regulations that cut across the different areas of digitalisation in the public sector, referencing good standards from other jurisdictions and enshrining digital rights.

However, considering the increasing expectations of citizens regarding public service delivery and the progressive use of emerging technologies such as artificial intelligence or the Internet of Things, some digital rights focused on personal data protection or digital security are quickly becoming insufficient. For instance, governments in OECD member countries are increasingly required to apply the "once-only principle" (i.e. citizens should provide the same information to the public sector only once), invest in proactive service delivery, secure data transparency and ownership or to open the algorithms applied on public decision-making processes. To keep improving its digital maturity, the Government of Lebanon should prioritise the development of these new generations of digital rights.

Political continuity and stability: The current political situation and the potential sustainability of the system in place and whether significant events could prevent the implementation and functioning of policies

Lebanon has been experiencing major civil demonstrations and political changes since October 2019. Despite the instability, there is a strong desire for government and digital reform from public and private stakeholders. The Lebanese Prime Minister Hassan Diab has committed to forming a government of independent technocrats to face the severe economic crisis in the country. With the current government approach that tries to keep the digital transformation draft strategy independent of the political cycle, there is a marginal guarantee for smooth and sustainable implementation and functioning of the policies and initiatives foreseen.

Federal or decentralised systems with higher levels of autonomy for administrative decision-making at the sub-national levels of government versus more centralised administrations: Decentralised states grant certain powers to local authorities, but retain control of the legality and the suitability of the administrative acts of regions with a measure of autonomy; a more centralised state ensures and guarantees to all citizens identical legislation throughout the territory by centralising power in one institution, with the autonomy of local authorities minimal

Lebanon is a highly centralised state and the Government of Lebanon is aware of the importance of centralisation and standardisation in its digital government and public services to improve economies of scale, expedite service delivery and ensure interoperability and good technical standards. The government should continue securing this centralised co-ordination through OMSAR to accelerate the digital government agenda and to design and implement efficient and coherent policies. Simultaneously, current centralised co-ordination efforts should also be used to progressively equip local governments with the necessary digital capacities that can enable more policy decentralised approaches in the future.

Local territories: The activity (and sometimes the whole system) in each area that serves a local population

Lebanon is divided into eight governorates, each considered to be an administrative division of the country, subdivided into 26 districts except for Beirut (see Figure 2.2). Lebanon's digital transformation draft strategy considers the need for the broadest participation of local governments. Private and public spaces across Lebanon should host an ecosystem where innovation can take place by fostering co-operation and collaboration between local governments, citizens and businesses. Local skills and contributions will thrive at community centres, innovation hubs and public venues. Co-ordination will be crucial to enable local governments and economies to keep up with the transformation.

Figure 2.2. Governorates in Lebanon

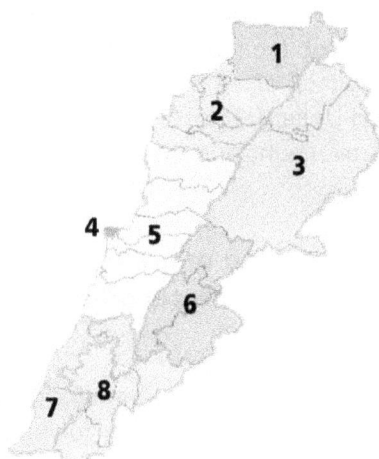

1	Akkar	عكّار
2	North Lebanon	الشمال
3	Baalbek-Hermel	بعلبك-الهرمل
4	Beirut	بيروت
5	Mount Lebanon	جبل لبنان
6	Beqaa	البقاع
7	South Lebanon	الجنوب
8	Nabatiyeh	النبطية

Source: (Lebanese Arabic Institute, 2020[2]), "Administrative Divisions of Lebanon", https://www.lebanesearabicinstitute.com/administrative-divisions-lebanon/.

Concentration versus dispersion of functions within institutions in charge of digitalisation as a tool to advance the maturity of digital government: Relationship between the various levels of the central body or the single and hierarchical structure in charge of digitalisation

According to Lebanon's digital transformation draft strategy, the institutions and government units in charge of digital government are organised in a top-down pyramidal structure. Specifically, the Ministerial Digital Transformation Committee (DEDTMC), the Digital Economy and Digital Transformation Steering Committee (DEDTSC), the Programme Management Office (PgMO), the Digital Transformation Unit (DTU), and implementation teams. This institutional model could be better organised in an efficient and agile way to streamline the co-ordination, oversight, strategy, standardisation and monitoring of it's the digital transformation (covered in Chapter 3 on Institutional Models). In order to better implement its digital government policy, the Government of Lebanon can consider reinforcing OMSAR's role as the public sector organisation in charge of the execution of the digital transformation draft strategy and supervise the operations of the Digital Transformation Units (DTUs). This should be achieved through the attribution of a clear and specific mandate, strong oversight and co-funding authority. It should also be backed by adequate financial and human capital.

Procurement versus commissioning of goods and services: The level of agility and dynamic of involvement of private stakeholders in the process of acquiring digital goods and services

Procurement is a key area of focus in Lebanon's digital transformation. The Government of Lebanon is making the effort to avoid pitfalls such as lack of budgets for sustainability and recurring costs. It is reviewing procurement laws and processes and looking to the implementation and use of efficient e-procurement. It has also made procurement a Key Performance Area (KPA 6.2) in order to expand the utilisation of public e-procurement activities across the Lebanese economy. It will also continue to engage in pre-commercial procurement to facilitate innovation, and partner with industry players to increase the share of the national ICT industry in public and donor-funded procurement. Under the legislation, the parliament has enacted the Public-Private Partnership Law that encapsulates modern public procurement procedures and practices and starts capacity building with public procurement. The Government of Lebanon has in place good strategies and approaches to the procurement of digital goods and services in an agile and dynamic way – covering funding, partnerships and training. In 2020, OMSAR launched its e-Procurement Platform that covers the full procurement cycle in an adaptable manner based on existing regulations and rules. It allows suppliers, contracts and consultants to participate freely in procuring in Lebanon. This platform can be easily transformed based on open data standards. However, rampant corruption may threaten the efficacy of procurement at an operational level. The Government of Lebanon should focus on the governance of the e-Procurement Platform and further digitalisation of procurement processes.

Dimension 2. Socio-economic factors

Socio-economic factors refer to "social and economic matters and their relations that can fundamentally determine, or influence, digital government priorities and the necessary mechanisms of governance to achieve a coherent and sustainable digital transformation of the public sector" (OECD, forthcoming[1]).

Overall economic climate: The country's economic condition and how it can determine the digital government policy

After reaching record growth levels between 2007 and 2010 of 8% on average, driven by the reconstruction programme that followed the civil war, Lebanese economic growth has slowed since 2011 due to internal political tensions and the conflict in Syria (World Bank, 2016[3]). Economic growth was expected to accelerate slightly in 2019 at 1.4% and 2020 at 2%, due to the resilience of the tourism and banking sectors. Nevertheless, the country is facing deepening economic challenges in recent years due to economic crises, the recent civil protests and the COVID-19 pandemic. It is presently facing a severe liquidity shock and is defaulting on its foreign currency debts. The Government of Lebanon understands the importance of using digital technologies to boost public industry and market intelligence for better economic policy planning and to promote the digital transformation of its public sector through the inclusion of citizens in the process of governance and improve public communications. The OECD Digital Government Survey of Lebanon shows that data analytics are being used to address a range of social and economic challenges across the government, to drive innovation and support evidence-based policymaking. The Government of Lebanon should continue to emphasise on developing economic intelligence for better policies.

Levels of digitalisation within the population and adoption of digital public services: The digital inclusiveness of a country's population and the potential digital divide, i.e. the gap between individuals, households, businesses and geographic areas at different socio-economic levels in terms of opportunities to access information and communication technologies (ICTs) and interact with public services

Building on high levels of access to the Internet by its population at 78.2% in 2017 (World Bank, 2017[4]), the Government of Lebanon has a plan aimed at increasing the digital skills of citizens to access public services available online. The digital assistance programme targets citizens who need help to perform more online activities. Based on the digital transformation draft strategy, the Government of Lebanon is planning to support co-ordinated activities from the civil society, universities, vocational training centres, non-governmental organisations and private companies to attract higher online engagement and transaction with public services. The Government of Lebanon will also offer training and capacity building to public servants and staff to gain digital skills that enable them to serve the citizens electronically. In line with these important priorities, the country should also consider reinforcing efforts underway to improve basic user digital skills across all segments of the population. The success of digitalisation of the government and public sector relies on how well digital public services are received by citizens and that no vulnerable group is excluded, and new forms of digital exclusions emerge. The journey towards digital inclusion and equality must encompass both the public service providers and users, to secure that the new opportunities created can benefit the most. OMSAR can play a co-ordination role in expanding digital inclusiveness.

Levels of adoption of e-commerce: Development of business and services of the digital economy, their use by the population and the impact on digital government policy

In 2019, the United Nations Conference on Trade and Development B2C E-Commerce Index ranked Lebanon the 68th out of 152 economies, where the ranking has dropped from 55th in 2017 to 63rd in 2018 (UNCTAD, 2019[5]). BlomInvest Bank found that Lebanese people mostly use e-commerce for banking services with the highest e-commerce usage rate for money transfers and online bill payments (BlomInvest Bank, 2015[6]). In 2019, the Government of Lebanon launched the Commercial Register and the Lebanese Government Common Portal project based on an open and interoperable platform as an attempt to improve the ease of doing business and investments in Lebanon. It addresses government data availability and interoperability such that digital businesses and services can be more easily developed. The platform also significantly assists the government administration in transacting with users via e-services. Building on the experience of Lebanese citizens using e-commerce and services and the substantial levels of digitalisation observed, the Government of Lebanon should continue its efforts towards the progressive digitalisation of public services, investing in citizen-driven approaches for its design and delivery. Especially in the period of the COVID-19 pandemic, the government can ride on the positive trends and opportunities for e-commerce development.

Levels of competitiveness and innovation in the country: The measure of the country's advantage or disadvantage creating new digital products and services, determining the potential of a collaboration of the government with the private sector and the level of expectations towards the digital government policy

Innovation is not currently part of the tradition of government bodies according to observations collected in the OECD fact-finding mission to Beirut in June 2019. Reinforced partnerships between both research institutions and local technology businesses could incorporate the very best of modern technology and digital technology to unlock creativity and ingenuity in providing creative public services based on shared networks, advanced technology and scalable business resources. Lebanon has made of innovation one of the pillars of its digital transformation draft strategy alongside people, processes and civic engagement. The country has identified three major innovation focuses: technology using a cloud-first policy, the establishment of common digital platforms and the rise of digital services. This demonstrates the government's commitment to intensify policy efforts in this critical area.

Digital skills in the public sector: The digital competencies and abilities required for a digitally prepared public workforce, including digital user skills, digital professional skills, complementary digital skills and digital management and leadership skills

The OECD fact-finding mission team found a consensus among the ecosystem of stakeholders about the need to improve the digital skills availability in the public sector. According to the digital transformation draft strategy, the Government of Lebanon is willing to develop the digital skills of its civil servants in the public sector. The government has the goal of training 20 000 civil servants on various digital services in five years. This will be backed up by the launch of a digital academy with online training courses to build and improve digital skills and competencies of citizens and civil servants. Such training should be strategic, evaluative and consider the nature of jobs in the Lebanese public sector, including all central government employees such as contractual employees, temporary employees and daily workers in addition to civil servants. In 2016, OMSAR had launched a large-scale e-learning project "Boost Yourself" for officials across the public sector to familiarise themselves with digital learning solutions. The project offered hundreds of courses in Information Technology and Microsoft Office in addition to management and soft skills. 2 871 public sector employees participated with 1 519 finishing at least three courses. Beyond the investments on the user and professional skills, the Government of Lebanon could also consider prioritising the development of digital talent and culture among the public workforce in order to build a digital mindset across the administration that understands the benefits and challenges of the digital transformation underway.

Public trust: The extent to which people hold a positive perception about the actions of their government and how this can influence the level of ambition or priorities of the digital government strategy

Lebanon is a country where there has not been much trust in public institutions for many years. The recent protests in 2019 and the beginning of 2020 called for an end to a political regime maintained by a governing elite. The Arab Barometer underlines that in 2019, less than 20% of the Lebanese trust the government and 96% believe that corruption is endemic (Gohsn, F. and S.E. Parkinson, 2019[7]). The Government of Lebanon has given itself the goal of building more public trust by accountability, fighting inequality, corruption and bribery and acting in the best interests and demands of its people for a better standard of living and increased facilities in the public sector. The implementation and use of neutral and secure digital tools for public and financial services will be beneficial and essential in the digital transformation draft strategy. A positive example is the deployment of Courts Automation software, data centres and infrastructure in 2018 in a bid to restore public trust in the Lebanese justice system by increasing efficiency and transparency in case management. Another important tool and process to be highlighted is the digital Appointment Mechanism for senior vacant positions in the public administrations that was created in 2012 to combat corruption in the form of favouritism or nepotism. Such digital tools should have an impact on Lebanon's public governance as they will support the administration to restore citizens' trust, help increase the country's digital economy, and create the foundations for improved well-being across the population.

Diversity: The wide range of cultural, linguistic, ethnic, religious and socio-economic characteristics in the population

The main characteristic of Lebanon is its diversity and complexity – there are officially 18 religious beliefs and approximatively 5 million inhabitants and almost a million of foreigners with a considerable number of ties to Palestine Authority and Syria. Social classes in Lebanon are relatively distinct, which are determined by wealth or socio-economic class rank. This plurality has led to different languages being spoken by the population and the government, namely English, French and Arabic, and traditions within institutions. Considering that digital government can improve transparency, accountability and efficiency, which can reinforce citizen trust in government, the political support and attribution of administrative, financial and human resources for the implementation of the digital transformation draft strategy can help to overcome diversity challenges in Lebanon.

Migration: Movement of the population within, out of and from countries

Migration to Lebanon is not a new phenomenon considering the country's history. The war in Syria has plunged the region into an unprecedented crisis and more than a million refugees came into Lebanon. The management of these migrations is mainly done by international organisations or non-governmental organisations established in the region and working in camps or specific offices. Migration is an essential point in the organisation of the country and its social fabric and should be properly considered in the government's digital government strategy due to their administrative and economic impacts (OECD, forthcoming[11]). The development of targeted digital services for different segments of the immigration population can help the Government of Lebanon manage the phenomenon and should be prioritised.

Dimension 3. Technological context

The technological context refers to all the elements relating to or involving technology, especially the technological innovations that comprise new products and processes and significant technological changes of products and processes. The technological context also considers changes in terms of infrastructure development in the country, such as the system of public works in a country, state or region, including roads, utility lines and public buildings.

Coverage and level of development of the digital infrastructures: The scope and availability of means and connectivity in a territory

The progress of establishing digital and telecommunications infrastructure has been relatively slow in Lebanon, with frequent claims of mismanagement, corruption and monopoly among the stakeholders. The Ministry of Telecommunication manages internet services in Lebanon, and there are three kinds of available services on the territory: dial-up, wireless Internet and ADSL. The country ranks 155th worldwide in terms of fixed broadband speeds and 27th in terms of mobile speed based on the 2020 Speedtest Global Index (Speedtest, 2020[8]). This is likely to serve as a roadblock for digitalisation. The Government of Lebanon has identified this area of need and placed the clear target for improving digital infrastructure. The progress will be monitored based on the United Nations Electronic Government Development Index

(EDGI) (S06-1. KPI-1), where one of the three composite measures is telecommunication connectivity measured by development status of telecommunication infrastructure. The other two are the provision of online services and human capacity.

Technological legacy of the public sector, integration of technology into governance and business processes and public sector innovation: Past and ongoing public sector measures and agenda regarding digitalisation, innovation in collaboration with the private sector

A notable shift in Lebanon occurred in 2002 when the government expressed the will to change the country's technical-oriented strategy to make it more user-oriented and people-centered, namely, citizen-centric and business-centric ((OMSAR, 2002[9])). The plan sought to go beyond statistics and processes by working towards the goal of changing and improving how the government works. The aim was to use the strategy as a springboard for the development of a novel, innovative and creative plan that could transform Lebanon's traditional old-fashioned government operations into a modern, realistic and applicable e-government model. Many key focus initiatives were suggested for execution over a three-year timeline and examined with relevant parties. A high-level plan of action has been developed, and the digital transformation draft strategy and action plan take this technological evolution into account. Policy efforts foreseen by the Lebanese digital government strategy can be expected to positively influence digital adoption and integration in the public sector and in the economy.

However, a common understanding was found during the fact-finding mission to Beirut in June 2019 that there is still room for improvement for how the Lebanese public sector embeds digital technologies for value creation. Lebanon ranks 99th in the 2018 United Nations eGovernment Development Index (EGDI), dropping slightly in its position since the first edition of the index in 2008 where the country was ranked 74th (UNDESA, 2018[10]). Many initiatives in Lebanon remain private sector-oriented and are backed up by financial institutions in banks. More governmental initiatives should be implemented with techniques used to tackle a range of social and economic challenges within the administration, to drive entrepreneurship and innovation, and to support evidence-based policymaking. In this sense, establishing private and public partnerships are crucial to achieving this goal. Several national programmes and consortiums have emerged in Lebanon due to a robust entrepreneurial scene. The National Advisory Council on Innovation and Entrepreneurship in Lebanon seeks to identify and recommend solutions to issues that are central to pushing the innovation revolution. The Council intends to allow entrepreneurs and businesses to grow a professional, internationally competitive workforce. A good example is the Lebanese Industrial Research Achievements Programme (LIRA), aimed at building active co-operation between industry, academia and research centres to address the research and development needs of the Lebanese industry, empowering the industrial sector with innovations that promote competitiveness and productivity, and achieving a transition from a welfare to a knowledge-based economy.

Dimension 4. Environmental and geographical considerations

Environmental and geographic considerations refer to "geographic elements that influence the territorial organisation and take into account the growing influence of the effects of climate change and related environmental priorities such as global warming on the economy as this can impact the digital government strategy" (OECD, forthcoming[1]).

Regional variances: The analysis of all disparities between regions of a territory

A 2017 report by the Lebanese Ministry of Finance and the United National Development Programme highlighted that regional disparities within Lebanon have been responsible for income inequality (MOF/UNDP, 2017[11]). The report also noted a direct relationship between the rate of urbanisation and inequalities. The current strategy by the Government of Lebanon could focus how income inequality affects digital penetration in some areas, and could include measures to strengthen efforts on digital skills training and digital talent development, to avoid the emergence of new forms of digital divides as the public sector progresses in the digitalisation its processes and services.

Geological risks and hazards: Events linked to the natural and human-related activities on the planet, such as natural disasters

Lebanon is a relatively small country with a territory of 10 452 km2. It faces low to moderate seismicity and is traversed by significant faults that have generated devastating historical earthquakes. The urbanised coastal strip, especially Beirut, where more than 40% of the Lebanese population lives with a large part of the economic, political and administrative activity, makes Lebanon one of the Mediterranean countries most exposed to seismic risk. The government is aware of that, and the digital transformation draft strategy considers this vulnerability owing to its geographical location, country size and very restricted access to international connectivity. Natural disasters, systemic problems and cyber attacks threaten the critical infrastructure, and put the systems and data in the country at risk. Although OMSAR suggests the necessity for a safe location outside the country to establish a disaster recovery location where the Government of Lebanon and private sector retain control of sensitive Lebanese data, this can only be done based on active co-operation with data management and storing firms and a stable political agreement with a country that would not undermine Lebanese interests. The Cloud-First policy should be built that way and taking external hazards into account (OMSAR, 2019[12]).

References

BlomInvest Bank (2015), *E-Commerce in Lebanon: Logging in to Potential*, [6]
https://blog.blominvestbank.com/wp-content/uploads/2015/03/E-Commerce-in-Lebanon-Logging-in-to-Potential-1.pdf.

Gohsn, F. and S.E. Parkinson (2019), *Lebanese protesters don't trust their government to* [7]
reform. Here's why., https://www.arabbarometer.org/media-news/lebanese-protesters-dont-trust-their-government-to-reform-heres-why/ (accessed on 25 May 2020).

Lebanese Arabic Institute (2020), *Administrative Divisions of Lebanon*, [2]
https://www.lebanesearabicinstitute.com/administrative-divisions-lebanon/ (accessed on 11 April 2020).

MOF/UNDP (2017), *Assessing Labor Income Inequality in Lebanon's Private Sector: Findings,* [11]
Comparative Analysis of Determinants, and Recommendations.

OECD (forthcoming), "OECD Digital Government Project: E-Leaders Governance Handbook", *E-* [1]
Leaders Task Force on Governance.

OMSAR (2019), *Lebanon Digital Transformation: Strategies to Actions (2020 – 2030), Office of the Minister of State for Administrative Reform, Republic of Lebanon, Beirut.*. [12]

OMSAR (2002), *E-Government Strategy for Lebanon – December 2002*, http://www.databank.com.lb/docs/E-Government%20Strategy%20for%20Lebanon-%20OMSAR-%20%202002.pdf. [9]

Speedtest (2020), *Speedtest Global Index: Global Speeds April 2020*, https://www.speedtest.net/global-index (accessed on 25 May 2020). [8]

UNCTAD (2019), *United Nations Conference on Trade and Development B2B E-Commerce Index 2019, UNCTAD Technical Notes on ICT For Development*, https://unctad.org/en/PublicationsLibrary/tn_unctad_ict4d14_en.pdf. [5]

UNDESA (2018), *2018 United Nations E-Government Survey*, https://www.unescap.org/sites/default/files/E-Government%20Survey%202018_FINAL.pdf. [10]

World Bank (2017), *Individuals using the Internet (% of population) - Lebanon, The World Bank Data*, https://data.worldbank.org/indicator/IT.NET.USER.ZS?locations=LB (accessed on 25 May 2020). [4]

World Bank (2016), *World Bank Group Country Survey (WBCS), Lebanon (LBN_2016_WBCS_v01_M).*, https://microdata.worldbank.org/index.php/catalog/2867/study-description. [3]

Chapter 3. Institutional models

Defined roles and responsibilities and a clear consensus on governance and operational objectives are essential prerequisites for a successful and effective digital transformation of the government and public sector. The mandate, representation and attributes that stakeholders assign to public sector organisations responsible for digital government policies are key aspects that need to be addressed when evaluating the current structural structures. The role of these institutions is essential in ensuring adequate governance and co-ordination of initiatives across all policy areas and government levels, in order to succeed in the transition from agency-thinking and government-centered methods to system-thinking and citizen-driven imperatives in policy making and delivery of public services (OECD, forthcoming[1]).

Institutional models profoundly shape countries' digital government agendas from design to implementation. Understanding and rolling out optimised institutional set-ups is crucial for effective and efficient implementation of digital government strategies. It demands co-ordination between a plurality of actors and processes and for this to be ensured institutions need to rely on standards, rules and procedures. The organisation of digital government institutions can be analysed through four major dimensions: 1) macro-structure of the government; 2) nature of the leading public sector organisation; 3) leadership model encompassing position and role; and 4) level of co-ordination and compliance (see Figure 3.1).

Figure 3.1. Digital government institutional models

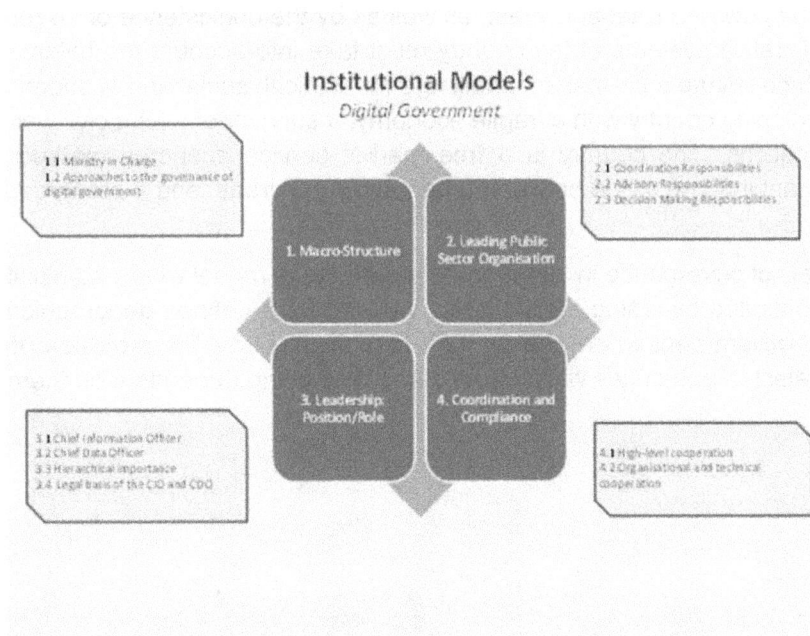

Note: CIO = Chief Information Officer; CDO = Chief Data Officer.
Source: (OECD, forthcoming[1]), OECD E-Leaders Governance Handbook.

Governments around the world are gradually adapting institutional settings to better lead the digitalisation of their public administrations. To accurately organise the digitalisation of the public sector, countries have established institutions to manage and co-ordinate digital government choices at the federal or national levels of state, often in the manner of units or branches within current organisations, directorates, agencies or even ministries.

The choice of the governance structure is not directly related to the level of digital government maturity of the country, or human and financial resources in the public sector. It is however important to underline that the position of the person in charge of the agency, department or unit in the central government responsible for digital government has a significant impact on the management ability and capacity to use digital technology to promote a more efficient, innovative, open, inclusive and sustainable public sector. The governance model assists the government in refining its perspective on the digital government and generating the financial capacity to drive enhancement through a coherent use of innovation.

The model should be implemented while considering the political framework of the country, its legal and administrative context, and the tradition of governance for digital government in a specific nation (OECD, forthcoming[1]). Given the recent political instability in Lebanon leading to an overhaul of the government and the political organisation of the country, it seems more judicious to study the institutional models under the prism of the elements put forward in the digital transformation draft strategy. Thus, this chapter will highlight the approach chosen by the Office of the Minister of State for Administrative Reform (OMSAR) by focusing on the following elements: the governance model, the structure, the designated roles and responsibilities and the subjects of co-ordination and compliance.

Lebanon's administrative organisation

Lebanon became independent from the Ottoman Empire and the French mandate in 1943. Consequently, the country retained the governmental systems and traditions of both Ottoman and French systems. The country benefits from wide cultural and religious diversity, demonstrated by its strategic location in the Middle East, as a link between East and West, as well as by the coexistence of 18 religious groups. The political and administrative systems of the country must take into account the balances and interests of those groups, which constitute a permanent challenge for political, social and economic stability. Lebanon is considered a developing country with a fragile economy, a survivor of a long civil war from 1975 to 1990 and ethnic confrontations. The country is a free market service economy marked by limited natural resources, a significant income divide between urban and rural areas, and a broad gap between rich and poor (AbouAssi, 2015[2]).

There are two models of governance in Lebanon: 1) a prefectural model where administrative services are co-ordinated and controlled by a single state agent working for a defined geographical area; 2) a model based on local self-government where the primary responsibility for the provision of public services is assigned to locally elected authorities while at the same time being dependent on them (see Figure 3.2).

Figure 3.2. Current sub-national administrative structure in Lebanon

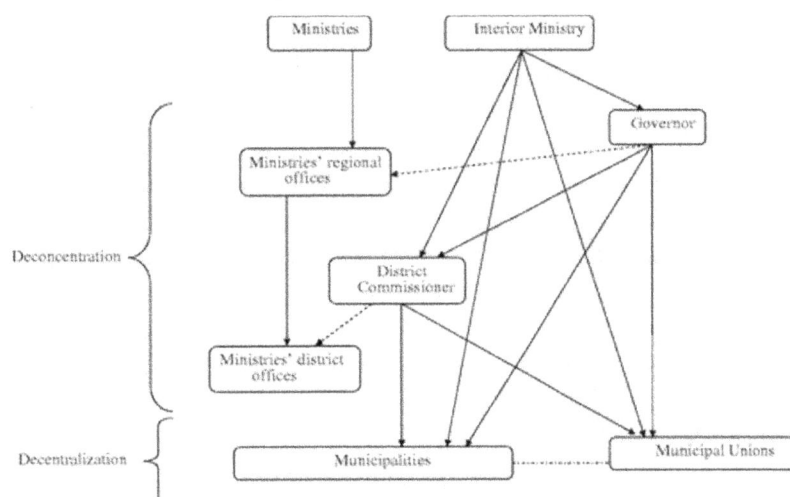

Source: (AbouAssi, 2015[2]), "Giving in Lebanon: Traditions and Reality in an Unstable Environment", https://doi.org/10.1057/978113734153_20.

Influenced by the French mandate, the devolution system has been in place since 1959 and has changed little since its introduction. Lebanon is divided into eight governorates (Muhafazat) and 26 districts (Qada), where the ministries are represented by regional offices and this corresponds to an integrated prefectural administrative structure. The various ministerial offices in the regions are chaired by an agent of the state, who liaises with the higher authorities. The governor (Muhafiz) exercises his functions at the governorate level and the representative (Qai'mmaqam) at the district level (Lebanese Arabic Institute, 2020[3]) (see Figure 3.3).

Figure 3.3. Districts of Lebanon

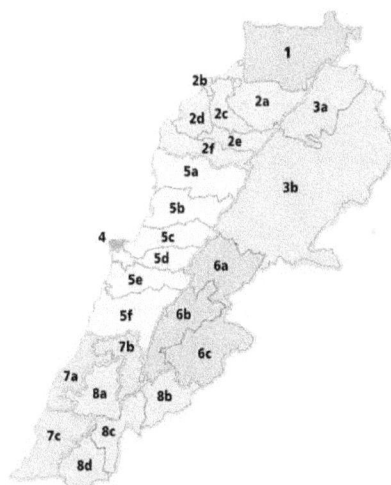

Note: Except for Beirut, each district is divided into municipalities. There were 1029 municipalities at the time of the 2016 municipal elections.
Source: (Lebanese Arabic Institute, 2020[3]), "Administrative Divisions of Lebanon", https://www.lebanesearabicinstitute.com/administrative-divisions-lebanon/.

The Lebanese civil war from 1975 to 1990 devastated the administrative infrastructure and froze government process for almost two decades. Government and civil procedures in Lebanon have been severely weakened. According to the stakeholders interviewed in the OECD fact-finding mission in June

2019, delay and maladjustment are numerous and touch almost the entire interface between the government and the daily life of citizens. This structural weakness constitutes an obstacle for the economic development, political and administrative system of the country today. In this sense, a digital transformation of the public sector supported by a clear and strong governance framework can support the Lebanese public sector to better respond to citizens and businesses expectations and needs.

OMSAR was created in 1994 for the purpose of administrative reform. The Council of Ministers at the time charged the Minister of State for Administrative Reform with the responsibility of co-ordinating efforts to set up this structure. The state ministry website declares the purpose of OMSAR is to develop the institutional and technical capacities of the Lebanese ministries, central bodies, public agencies and municipalities. OMSAR is in charge of: 1) assessing their reform and development needs; 2) devising and updating administrative reform and e-Government strategies; 3) identifying, implementing and evaluating development projects that translate the strategies into action; 4) conducting organisational and legal studies; 5) streamlining work procedures and training civil servants. OMSAR is keen to remain responsive to the demands of the Lebanese administrations and to modernise them by building effective partnerships with them as well as with international donors, non-government organisations and the civil society (OMSAR, 2019[4]). When it was established, OMSAR aimed to unify and computerise all administrative processes that individuals could perform or order the issuing of civil status documents or the payment of taxes. Such regulatory overhaul has the official benefit of saving people time and money for administrative processes by computerised operations.

Figure 3.4. Lebanon's digital transformation journey

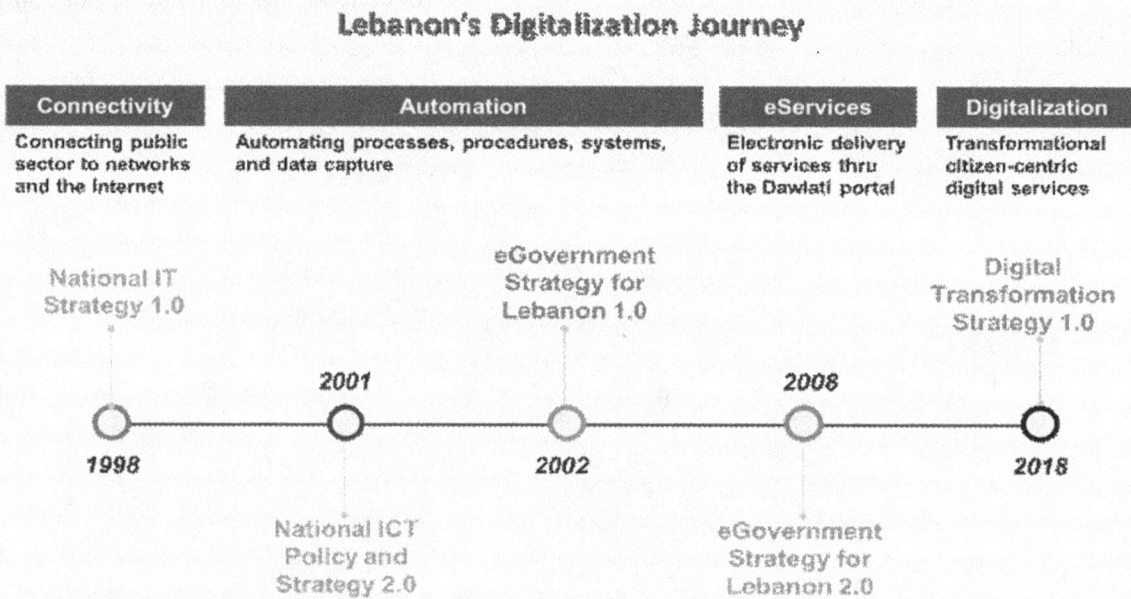

Source: (OMSAR, 2019[4]), Lebanon Digital Transformation: Strategies to Actions (2020 – 2030).
Lebanon's digital transformation governance

Lebanon is currently re-adjusting its political and institutional structures according to socio-economic conditions to meet citizen's and businesses' expectations better. Public governance is a critical issue for Lebanon and is presently under reform. This requires the establishment of a transparent governance model that provides a high level of political commitment, leadership, management and co-ordination. In addition to this, the governance model should consider the digital transformation of the public sector in the context of continuously evolving technologies. A public sector institutional model that cuts across organisational silos and promotes partnerships must be established. This model should enable clear leadership of the digital transformation policy and ensure inter-governmental co-ordination. Moreover, it must enable strengthened steering and co-ordination of activities within the approved digital transformation projects and hold teams accountable for the delivery of set actions within the action plan.

Lebanon has high aspirations and has made considerable strides in digitalising the country since OMSAR was formed in 1994 (see Figure 3.4). Nevertheless, in their efforts to promote creativity and move the digital transformation of the public sector to the next stage of digitalisation, the country faces implementation obstacles such as an insufficient governance structure to reach the desired transition. Stimulating digitalisation at the national level includes a comprehensive national digital strategy – a strategy that targets high and sets the technology agenda for all stakeholders with a whole of government approach. Lebanon's digital transformation draft strategy is based on five pillars: 1) people; 2) innovation; 3) processes; 4) civic engagement; and 5) legal framework. These five pillars encompass essential points that are part of the institutional models and policy levers identified by the Secretariat in line with the OECD Recommendation on Digital Government Strategies (see Figure 3.5). The critical components of each pillar will be analysed throughout this chapter.

Figure 3.5. Lebanon's proposed digital transformation pillars

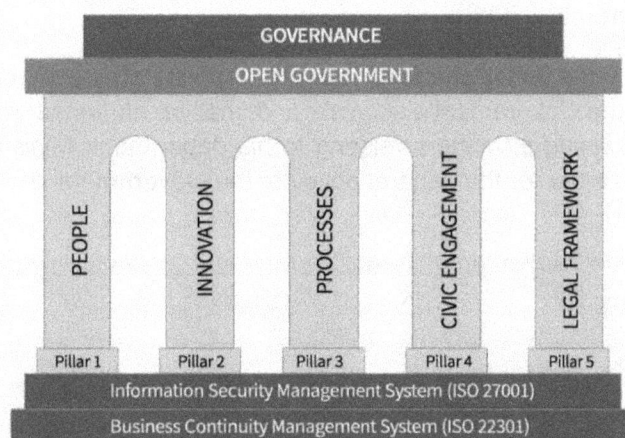

Source: (OMSAR, 2019[4]), Lebanon Digital Transformation: Strategies to Actions (2020 – 2030).

In reference to the structure of the E-Leaders Governance Handbook (OECD, forthcoming[1]), the following sections will be dedicated to analysing the dimensions and sub-dimensions of institutional models. The analysis will start by focusing on the institutional macrostructure, followed by the leading public sector organisation, the leadership position and role, and the co-ordination and compliance in place.

Dimension 1. Macro-structure

Article 66 of the Lebanese Constitution empowers each minister to lead and manage his or her ministry (see Box 3.1). Approaches cannot be enforced on the public administration until co-ordination and communication are assured, allowing the process of digital change to continue and proceed (Oueidat, 2018[5]). A sound governance model will facilitate appropriate and timely joint decision-making, thus helping to anticipate and avoid problems before they have a significant impact on the roadmap set by the stakeholders. Also, the governance model needs to ensure priorities are set so that actions are aligned to shared objectives and duplication of efforts is avoided. The model foreseen in the Lebanon digital transformation draft strategy addresses three levels of governance (see Figure 3.6), which are determined by the existing organisation of the Government of Lebanon and technological and organisational maturity of the institutions that will be included in the digital transformation implementation roadmap (OMSAR, 2019[4]). The following are the three levels of governance:

- The "strategy" level imparts authority on the digital transformation draft strategy within the government. The body with this degree of accountability will be responsible for the life cycle of all technology development and their continuous improvement.

- The "build" level involves the governance and possession of the technical and operational building blocks of the digital transformation draft strategy. The bodies with this degree of governance are responsible for the design of the building blocks of the digital transition structures as well as the maintenance of the activities.

- The "operate" level encompasses incorporation, administration and control of operations. This level of government is delegated to the public sector organisations responsible for the public services delivery.

Box 3.1. Article 66 of the Constitutional of Lebanon (amended by the Constitutional Law of 17 October 1927 and 21 September 1990)

Only Lebanese who satisfy the conditions for becoming deputies may assume ministerial posts. The Ministers shall administer the Government's services and shall be entrusted with appying the laws and regulations, each one pertaining to matters relating to his department. Ministers shall be collectively responsible before the Chamber for the general policy of the Government and individually responsible for their personal actions.

Source: (WIPO, 1990[6]), Constitution of Lebanon, https://www.wipo.int/edocs/lexdocs/laws/en/lb/lb018en.pdf.

Figure 3.6. Digital transformation strategy governance model

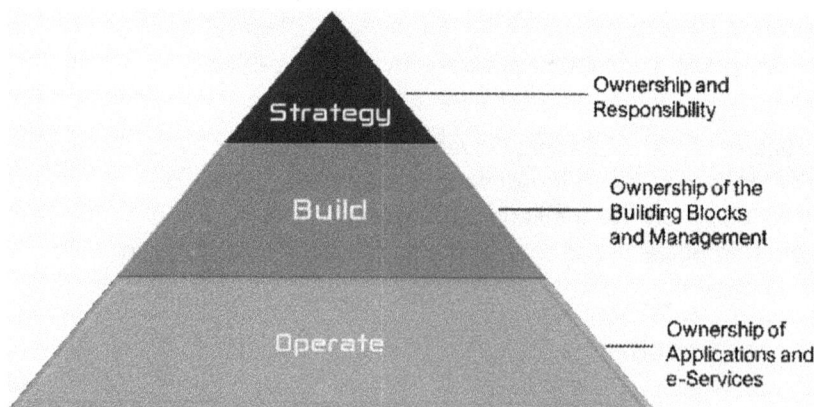

Source: (OMSAR, 2019[4]), Lebanon Digital Transformation: Strategies to Actions (2020 – 2030).

The governance model and its principles created by OMSAR (see Table 3.1) rely similarly on what is commonly referred to as good governance principles in public governance: comprehensive, open, shared, flexible and collaborative, which are like the standards of the European Union on governance: openness, participation, accountability, effectiveness and coherence (European Commission, 2001[7]).

Table 3.1. OMSAR's governance model principles

Comprehensive	All activities within and surrounding the performance of the delivered solution whether technological, administrative, or legal will fall within the scope of this governance model.
Open	The governance model shall facilitate an open dialogue amongst the stakeholders at all levels of the relationship.
Shared	The governance model requires 'buy-in' from all parties and shall align the goals set in the digital strategy and implementation plan.
Flexible	Over time, stakeholders can review and modify the governance model as appropriate in response to changing requirements, e.g. new scope.
Collaborative	The governance model will provide a framework for close collaboration that will build trust and respect amongst the stakeholders.

Source: (OMSAR, 2019[4]), Lebanon Digital Transformation: Strategies to Actions (2020 – 2030).

In terms of governance structure, Lebanon digital transformation draft strategy has proposed a top-down multi-level pyramidal structure allowing cross-governmental decision and implementation due to the organisation of the country (see Figure 3.7). The main idea of the strategy showcased in the implementation plan is to insert in each ministry specific units for the implementation of projects related to the digital transformation.

Figure 3.7. Proposed governance structure for digital government

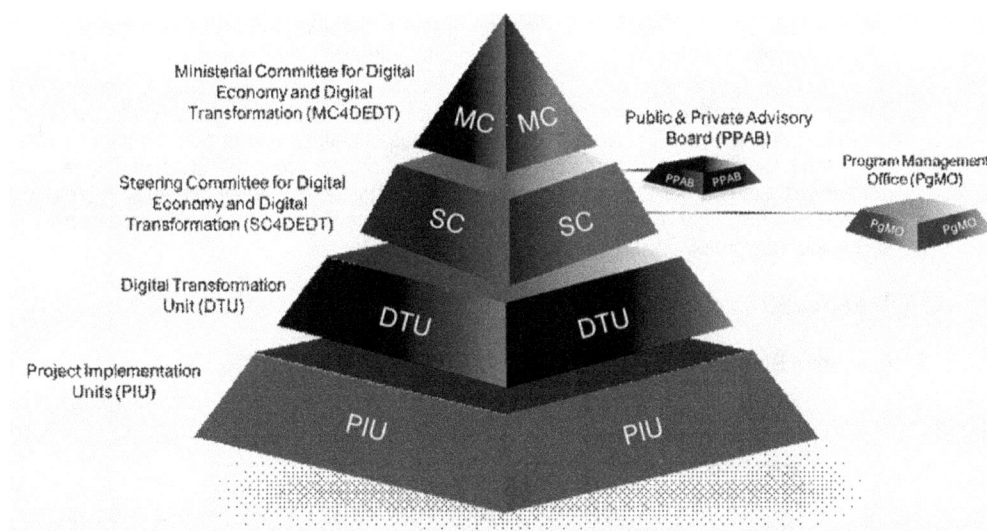

Source: (OMSAR, 2019[4]), Lebanon Digital Transformation: Strategies to Actions (2020 – 2030).

Table 3.2. Bodies in the Government of Lebanon's governance structure

Governance Body	Roles and Responsibilities
Ministerial Committee for Digital Economy and	This committee was formed by a decree from the Prime Minister of Lebanon. It consists of ministers responsible for driving the digital transformation in Lebanon and accountable for its success. The MC4DEDT responsibilities are:

Digital Transformation (MC4DEDT)	• Political and high-level commitment to the digital transformation vision and goals
	• High-level guidance and strategic decision making in alignment with the digital transformation draft strategy and action plan
	• Support and oversight of the overall digital transformation plan including (a) Portfolio of Programmes and Projects, (b) Priorities, (c) Budget, (d) Time Frame, (e) Resources, and (f) Key Performance Indicators (KPI)
	• Conduct periodic reviews of the overall status of programmes and projects delivered by the Steering Committee for Digital Economy and Digital Transformation (SC4DEDT) and monitor their progress and alignment with strategic objectives
	• Co-ordinate actions and issues with the Council of Ministers and the Lebanese Parliament to ensure collaboration between various government ministries
	• Manage potential political influences
	• Resolve escalated and complex issues, as necessary
	• Approve the project governance and appoint the Steering Committee for Digital Economy and Digital Transformation and all key positions related to the action plan
	• Instruct the Audit Unit to conduct ad hoc or periodic audit functions
	• Appoint the Public and Private Advisory Board (PPAB)
	• Dispute resolution, if raised by the SC4DEDT
	• Review periodically the overall project status delivered by the SC4DEDT
	• Meet every two months
	The MC4DEDT is chaired by the Prime Minister.
Steering Committee for Digital Economy and Digital Transformation (SC4DEDT)	The Steering Committee for Digital Economy and Digital Transformation (SC4DEDT) is chaired by the Prime Minister and was formed by a decision of the Prime Minister Decision 122 dated July 5, 2019. The SC4DEDT consists of programme directors and directors-general from key ministries involved in the digital transformation, appointed by their respective ministers.
	The Lebanon Digital Transformation consists of a portfolio of programmes, with each programme consisting of one or more projects owned by various ministries and/or public sector entities, and with each project varying in complexity and scope. Consequently, the SC4DEDT is responsible for managing the portfolio of programmes to ensure their adequate alignment with the overall strategy and oversight over programme implementations to ensure their intended goals and successful outcomes.
	The SC4DEDT has two main functions:
	Executive Sponsorship
	• Support: Provide executive support for all digital transformation programmes to increase chances of success and reduce resistance to change among the multitude of departments and stakeholders.
	• Funding: Ensure adequate funding is allocated for the various programmes in the portfolio.
	• Risk Mitigation: Identify risks, issues, and dependencies, and find solutions to achieve the overall objectives and keep the programmes on track.
	• Co-ordination: Co-ordinate with the Programme Management Office (PgMO) to ensure the right support and standards are being implemented across all programmes and projects.
	• Conflict Resolution: Resolve conflicts as they are escalated by the PgMO.
	• Oversight: Conduct bi-weekly meetings with the PgMO to review project plans, statuses, and discuss escalations requiring intervention.

	Portfolio Management ● Strategy: Ensure all programmes across the public sector are executed in unison to achieve the strategy set by the MC4DEDT. ● Prioritization: Focus mainly on doing the right work for the entire portfolio of digital transformation programmes and projects compared to the PgMO that focuses on doing the work right. Approve and submit projects for approval to the MC4DEDT. ● Monitoring: Measure the impact of the projects as they produce deliverables for providing feedback and ensuring continuous improvements. Based on the request of the MC4DEDT and a regular basis, conduct audit functions related to programmes and projects: ● Project Audit: Timeline, deliverables, resources, risks, and issues. ● Financial Audit: Verify that projects are in line with budgets. ● Legal Audit: Ensure compliance with governmental rules and regulations.
Public & Private Advisory Board (PPAB)	The members of this board are advisors from the public and private sectors, academia, director generals, and subject matter experts in the various fields. This group brings specific knowledge and skills that augment the knowledge and skills of the MC4DEDT, to effectively guide the digital transformation journey. Entities to consider for membership in the PPAB include the National Council for Entrepreneurship and Innovation (NCEI) and the Lebanese Economic Organization (LEO). The PPAB: ● Does not have a formal authority to govern, that is, the advisory committee cannot issue directives or decrees; the PPAB can only offer advice, make recommendations, and provide key information and materials ● Plays an important civic engagement and public relations role ● Provides a fresh perspective on programmatic issues ● Serves as an important complement to the effectiveness of both the MC4DEDT and the SC4DEDT as they carry out a specific initiative The main responsibilities of the PPAB are: ● Supporting the SC4DEDT in an advisory capacity ● Advising the Programme Management Office (PgMO) and Digital Transformation Unit (DTU) on action plans
Programme Management Office (PgMO)	The PgMO members consist of various stakeholders, from within the public sector, whose function is to manage, plan, and monitor programmes. The PgMO resides at OMSAR and acts as the leading hub for all digital transformation programmes and projects. The core functions of the PgMO are: ● Define, develop, and update government strategy and action plan for digital transformation ● Conduct project feasibility and assessment ● Survey all stakeholders and collect requirements for digital transformation projects ● Co-ordinate and monitor programme and project progress while ensuring alignment of the project implementations with the digital transformation strategic objectives ● Produce guidance, standards, and best practice that helps DTUs with their digital transformation efforts across the project lifecycles ● Support and provide programme planning and prioritization of projects and activities

	<ul><li>Manage the portfolio of programmes to ensure their adequate alignment with the overall strategy and oversight of programme implementations to ensure their intended goals and successful outcomes</li><li>Provide common project management tools to support DTUs</li><li>Provide support mechanisms for cross-functional teams to integrate and use these tools</li><li>Provide training and facilitate project management, mentoring, and coaching</li><li>Provide support through local and international expertise for digital transformation projects</li><li>Support the development of right digital skills and culture to transform public services</li><li>Conduct post-mortems/capture, communicate, and incorporate lessons learned</li><li>Provide change management, procedure simplifications, and process re-engineering</li><li>Support, develop and provide KPIs aligned with strategic objectives</li><li>Reporting to the SC4DEDT</li></ul>
Digital Transformation Units (DTU)	The members of these units will be a mixture of specialists within each of the public sector organizations. Each public administration entity will have a co-ordinator representing his or her organization to co-ordinate with the PgMO. The DTU responsibilities are:<ul><li>Lead the technical implementations of the digital transformation draft strategy and action plan</li><li>Ensure standardization of shared digital-by-design e-services and common platforms to improve economies of scale and expedite delivery with the help of PgMO</li><li>Co-ordinate and follow up on the progress of all the projects with DTUs established within other ministries and public sector entities</li><li>Provide technical oversight over the various digital transformation tasks and activities</li><li>Provide technical oversight over the implementation team</li><li>Escalating any major issues or risks to the PgMO</li></ul>
Project Implementation Units (PIU)	The Project Implementation Units (PIU) shall consist of various thematic groups. These groups contain various teams working on various projects simultaneously. Each thematic group will have its role based on its expertise:<ul><li>The Legal & Organizational Thematic group has the role and responsibility for co-ordinating all legal and organizational aspects of the Digital Transformation including:<ul><li>Participation in drafting necessary legal instruments and adjustments of existing ones</li><li>Operational instructions</li><li>Organizational adjustments</li><li>Organizational change management</li></ul></li><li>The Technical Thematic Group consists of project managers and comparable profiles performing implementation and related activities as part of the overall effort. Their responsibilities are:<ul><li>Implementing projects residing in their corresponding public entities</li><li>Co-ordinating all related activities</li><li>Synchronizing inter-related tasks to reach common goals and facilitate communication with external stakeholders and institutions, when needed</li></ul></li></ul>

	• Co-ordination of development of training programmes and training of affected stakeholder employees and citizens
	• Reporting to the DTU, regularly and frequently
	• Escalating any major issues or risks to the DTU
	• Facilitating the approval and endorsement of key deliverables

Source: (OMSAR, 2019[4]), Lebanon Digital Transformation: Strategies to Actions (2020 – 2030).

The institutional model framed in the digital transformation draft strategy of Lebanon seems to accommodate the need of political support through the MC4DEDT, the required steering across different public sector stakeholders foreseen through the SC4DEDT, the involvement of the ecosystem of stakeholders to be secured by the PPAB and the concrete implementation needs through the PgMO, DTU and PIU (see Table 3.2). In this sense, considering the institutional challenges observed by the OECD fact-finding team in the mission to Beirut in June 2019, the existence of an institutional model that can strengthen the coherency and sustainability of the digital government policy is a decisive step that demonstrates the Lebanese government commitment to enhance the digital transformation underway.

To obtain the highest possible and required governance maturity, the Lebanese government should consider the following risks:

1. New institutional models versus building on the existing ones: Although several merits can be pointed to, the development of an institutional model from start instead of building on an existing one can generate further resistance from the stakeholders involved. It would in fact require the establishment of a culture of institutional collaboration with new rules and practices. The Government of Lebanon should strongly invest in the concrete adoption by the public sector of the new institutional model foreseen. Otherwise, there is a high risk of problems emerging regarding its effective functioning.

2. Complex models versus simple models: The complexity of public governance requires institutional models that can secure political support, leadership, co-ordination and implementation capacities. The sustainability of an institutional model to manage the existing complexity depends on the capacity to be acknowledged, apprehended and supported by the ecosystem. As such, simplicity is a key asset. The Government of Lebanon should explore ways to simplify the institutional models foreseen in the digital transformation draft strategy.

Dimension 2. Leading public sector organisation

In various OECD countries, the leadership of public sector organisations responsible for the digital government is an essential tool for change in the public sector. It is fundamental for such public sector organisations in-charge of digital government to take on a clear leadership role on digital government policies for coherence, standardisation and sustainability of government efforts, especially in a disruptive context of rapid and constant technological evolution. The type of public sector organisation in place or required to lead the digital government policy is a critical governance dimension to be analysed and the experience of OECD countries is quite diverse in this domain (see Box 3.2).

In Lebanon, the Ministerial Committee for Digital Economy and Digital Transformation (MC4DEDT) should play a co-ordination role to OMSAR that leads strongly in the implementation and supervision of the digital transformation draft strategy. The Government of Lebanon currently misses the existence of an entity responsible for leading and co-ordinating decisions on digital government at central or federal level, which affects policy implementation. To fill this gap, the Government of Lebanon foresees the creation of a Lebanese Digital Agency within OMSAR in its digital transformation draft strategy. The mentioned institutional option of creating a Lebanese Digital Agency follows the experience of OECD countries such as the United Kingdom's Digital Government Service (DGS), Australia's Digital Transformation Agency (DTA), Portugual's Agency for Administrative Modernisation (AMA) and Italy's Agency for Digital Italy (AGID). The foreseen creation of the Lebanese Digital Agency within OMSAR can represent a decisive step to improve the maturity of the digital government policy in the country, allowing the allocation of resources and improving implementation capacities across the admnistration. In the case of Lebanon, where progress is very heterogeneous according to the different levels of government, an organisation of this kind could allow better monitoring and evaluation of the implementation suited to the different policy areas and levels of government of the Lebanese public sector with adequate responsibilities.

Nonetheless, given the administrative and civil uncertainty in the country, the Government of Lebanon is facing a critical moment with limited time and resources. It is therefore highly recommended that the Government of Lebanon first consider reinforcing the mandate and strengthening capacity of OMSAR in digital government co-ordination and implementation. Considering the implications associated with the establishment of a new public sector organisation like administrative actions, compliance costs, recruitment of staff, definition of internal procedures, substantive allocation of resources and changes in the institutional model in place, the decision should be taken when all the other alternatives have been considered. The reinforcement of the mandate of OMSAR and its capacities for implementation through proper policy levers (see Chapter 5 on Policy Levers) could be a better alternative to be explored by the Government of Lebanon.

Box 3.2. Types of digital government bodies

Internal unit, office or directorate: Units, departments or directorates in the centre of government or powerful ministries of co-ordination generally have a proper planning ability and understanding of the political agenda of the state. Experience across OECD countries shows varying amounts of the budget allocated to the department accountable for organising digital government (as a percentage of public spending). Administrative assistance and appropriate economic assets must, have course, be assigned to the Unit/Directorate for this organisational structure to bring about a significant shift in administration, as was the situation in the United Kingdom. In 2015, more than GBP 58 million was obtained by the Government Digital Service of the United Kingdom, for a sum of 0.01 % of government spending. However, this sort of framework appears to be very susceptible to policy changes and the evolving objectives of its supervisory minister.

Agency: Digital government agencies are characterised by stabilisation of their staff and management, stronger financing and higher independence from policy processes and objectives. They can be either merely managerial or can include influential policy-making and supervisory capabilities. In instances where legislative support functions have not been allocated to the agency, a powerful ministry and a healthy operating relationship at the upper leadership stage can account for this absence of authority, as the Ministry may be susceptible to embrace the laws suggested by the agency. The agency's ability to implement these laws and its political backing and credibility are crucial to ensure the efficiency of its job. This organisational set-up increases the trade-off between political power and the executive agency's autonomy. Despite its greater independence from the political cycle, a radical failure to observe political considerations vis-à-vis the current ecosystem could lead to a failure of administrative assistance, which would significantly diminish its capacity to drive digital transformation.

Ministerial or similar ranking authority: Nations with Ministers, Secretaries of State, Deputy Ministers or Under-Secretaries performing the duties of Government CIOs shall be drawn into account in this categorisation. For the sake of simplification, this evaluation would apply to these instances as ministerial or comparable classification political authorities. These institutions provide a compelling vision and financing for the digital government initiative and strengthen the political and policy-making authority of the organisation responsible for this strategy. However, this organisational set-up poses the danger of uncertainty in its governance and absence of continuity in its strategy and objectives. Besides, political factors may bias evidence-based preferences in favour of more apparent objectives.

Source: (OECD, 2016[8]), Digital Government in Chile: Strengthening the Institutional and Governance Framework, https://dx.doi.org/10.1787/9789264258013-en.

Another important governance variable to be analysed is the institutional location of the public sector organisation leading the digital government in the government ministerial structure. Among OECD countries, the organisations in control of the digital government policy are situated either in the centre of government, in a co-ordinating ministry or in a line ministry (see Box 3.3). Countries that have their public sector organisations in charge of the digital transformation draft strategy at the centre of government generally represent and secure the commitment of the highest political level to the new governance agenda, the advantages of the political power that radiates from the centre of the policy decision, and a more exceptional ability to integrate the vision into the broader plan for public sector modernisation. Strong executive power and support for the digital transformation of the public sector is a good reason to put the digital government body/unit at the centre of government.

Box 3.3. Types of structures

Centre of Government: Corresponds to the administrative framework that is working under and constitutes the Executive power (President, Prime Minister, and the Executive Cabinet as a whole). It has a wide range of titles across nations, such as the General Secretariat, Cabinet Office, Chancellery, Office or Ministry of the Presidency, the Office of the Council of Ministers. In many nations, the centre of government consists of more than one device, performing distinct tasks. One of its primary tasks is to ensure that public policies are enforced.

Co-ordinating Ministry: Overarching ministry responsible for general public administration matters, managing policies or instruments that crosscut the public sector. The Ministry of Finance, the Ministry of Public Administration or the Ministry of Planning are relevant examples to be considered.

Line Ministry: Government ministry in charge of a specific policy area, as compared to the co-ordinating ministries that are responsible for overall planning and matters of public administration. Ministry of ICT, Ministry of Science and Technology or Ministry of Innovation are typical examples of lie ministries that might lead the digital government policy.

Source: (OECD, 2016[8]), Digital Government in Chile: Strengthening the Institutional and Governance Framework, https://dx.doi.org/10.1787/9789264258013-en.

Nevertheless, the governance system described above may be more vulnerable to political influence than others and continues to face pressure for success and the political capitalisation of outcomes. Considering the current political situation in Lebanon, it is essential to ensure the operational stability of these governance arrangements, to align strategic assistance and commitment with the long-term viability of choices (OECD, 2016[8]); (OECD, forthcoming[1]).

The cross-cutting complexity of digital government has driven several OECD countries to set up the lead institutional body/unit under co-ordinating ministries such as the Ministry of Public Administration or the Ministry of Finance, thereby providing a mechanism for establishing ties between the digital government policy and the broader public sector reform agenda and policy goals. In other cases, this entity or organisation responds to a line ministry responsible for policy streams such as economic affairs or digital technologies in a broad sense. This option can lead to good policy outcomes if the mentioned ministry is properly recognised as leading this policy area by other ministries and manages important policy levers such as the management of ICT investments for instance (see Chapter 4 on Policy Levers).

The creation of Ministerial Committee for Digital Economy and Digital Transformation (MC4DEDT) by a Prime Minister decree in June 2019 reflects the support of the higher branch of the Lebanese executive power for the establishment of a decision-making institution in charge of the strategy's organisation. The location of the MC4DEDT at the centre of government, securing the necessary straight co-ordination with OMSAR that is part of the Ministry of Administrative Reform, encourages and facilitates the cross-cutting value of digital government policy across the public sector. Given the far-reaching reforms undertaken by Lebanon in several sectors and industries that bring digital transformation into play, it seems appropriate to follow the approach in place. The primary issue is whether the co-ordination benefits from the political stability to act as a driver of transformation within the administration. If the support of newly established executive power follows, strong conditions will be in place for the proper implementation of the strategy.

Dimension 3. Leadership: Position/role

The need for leadership and co-ordination across the public sector on digital government policies has led to the creation of specific positions to officiate, recognise and designate a body or person-in-charge. Several countries have established a position of an officer in charge of leading the definition and implementation of the digital transformation draft strategy. In many countries this has resulted in the creation of the Government Chief Information Officer (CIO) position at the national level, with natural variants on the designation and position title adopted from country to country to help ensure the effective and sustainable execution of the digitalisation policy in collaboration with the various stakeholders, from the public sector, business and start-up players, and the civil society.

The role of the CIO usually requires a variety of responsibilities. The CIO can be responsible for overseeing the implementation plans of the national strategy, suggest the adjustment of the policy priorities as necessary, and advocate for new policies and regulations that encourage digitalisation. The CIO can also contribute to the establishment of useful metrics for the evaluation and application of digitalisation across the entire ecosystem. The CIO could play a leading role in promoting the best practice of connectivity and sustainability through the new engagement of people so as not to reinvent the wheel over and over. Finally, the CIO can also help to address the lack of technical expertise, both at the level of execution and the level of leadership, as some specialisation sectors can only be defined on a large scale.

Lebanon does not have a permanent CIO and OMSAR lacks advisory and decision-making powers in the digital transformation process. The digital transformation draft strategy of Lebanon mentions the role of CIOs, but their role is not described and no details are given about their functions, position and duties (OMSAR, 2019[4]). Having an official CIO located at OMSAR or considering this role to be played by the head of the foreseen agency in charge of the strategy's application would be relevant to secure coherency and co-ordination across the whole government. The establishment of a CIO could also improve responsibility and accountability in the digital transformation strategy implementation in the whole ecosystem of digital government stakeholders.

A similar position progressively being adopted by different OECD countries is the Chief Data Officer (CDO), the person-in-charge of data governance in the government of the country (see Box 3.4). This status highlights the fact that data is perceived to be an essential and critical resource for the digital development of the country (OECD, 2019[9]). In turn, the development of an integrated global enterprise-wide plan for data governance and the design of data-driven facilities and institutions helps to avoid separation of organisational systems, creates a culture of communication between civil servants and provides competitive, scalable solutions and facilities intended for collaboration between individuals, businesses and civil society.

Box 3.4. The emerging role of the chief data officer

Many OECD countries are establishing a chief data officer position at the central government level. As this phenomenon becomes more widespread, the question that remains to be addressed concerns to what extent the chief data officer (CDO) position overlaps or complements that of the chief information officer (CIO). Normally, the role of the CIO is to manage the public sector's or an agency's use of technology to fulfil its mission. From this perspective, there is almost always an overlap between data and technology because technology is used to produce, store and transmit data. In other ways, it is different. The CIO should be data-informed, but modern CIOs responsible for designing and co-ordinating the implementation of Digital Government Strategies are tasked with a mandate that is broader within an organisation than gathering, managing, publishing or analysing data. At the level of national government and agencies, CIOs are juggling multiple responsibilities beyond data warehousing, from security to data centres.

The CDO plays the crucial role of a visionary and compelling leader. The rise of CDOs in the 21st century reflects the central role that data now plays in every facet of society. CDOs are entrusted not just with managing information but going one layer deeper in the knowledge generation and management process to raw data creation, collection, storage, sharing and analysis. In an increasing number of organisations, a CDO's position is established with the expectation that he/she collaborates with the CIO tasked with managing the digital government strategies and IT infrastructure at a government agency to ensure that data are available for organisational needs and to support strategic decisions, instruments and techniques, to account for the usually insufficient ICT capabilities of most public facilities. The approach of this model is aimed at finding "fast gains" for improving service quality to ensure the necessary amount of administrative assistance. However, this disruptive strategy may encounter problems with longer-term organisational and economic shift across the government due to their external position and culture.

Source: (OECD, 2016[8]), Digital Government in Chile: Strengthening the Institutional and Governance Framework, https://dx.doi.org/10.1787/9789264258013-en.

A common approach is a critical success factor in promoting better data governance that offers the foundation for defined positions and duties and government-wide leadership on the data-driven platform. Only a minority of nations countries having a Chief Data Officer (CDO) at the central/federal public stage in 2014, while the amount of OECD countries that established this role improved significantly in 2016 (OECD, 2019[9]). Lebanon emphasises a reasonably large part for data management in the country's digital transformation draft strategy. For instance, OMSAR is developing the platform for open data which should be managed by the Central Administration of Statistics (CAS). Strong priority is also attributed in the digital transformation draft strategy to boost data exchange across the public sector through common interoperability standards. In this sense, the government of Lebanon should consider institutionalising the position of CDO to be placed within OMSAR or in the foreseen agency that would be responsible for the implementation of the digital government policy. This would allow better management of the government's data policy and could support the development of partnerships related to the use and external storage of Lebanese data.

Many countries around the globe are still trying to come up or consider the establishment of a CIO/CDO function. Nevertheless, while the concept of a critical presence of a CIO or a similar role for the central government is almost universal across OECD countries, the degree of the CIO in the organisational structure of the government to which it reports, its function and policy mechanisms are essential factors for its success in guiding change in public administration. In addition to defining and implementing a national digital policy plan, CIO/CDO need to work on creating an environment that allows it to be enforced, striving to engage key stakeholders, leveraging their influence and facilitating effective alliance-building mechanisms.

Dimension 4. Co-ordination and compliance

Sound governance requires excellent co-ordination and commitment from the leadership and its units. In addition to effective organisational and governance frameworks, there is a need to establish reliable knowledge sharing and technical co-operation at the governmental level and with international bodies. A favourable operating climate to advance the digital transformation provides a stronger link between digital policy initiatives and broader policy objectives that positively strengthen people's trust in the public sector and the capacity to leverage digital government towards improved social well-being and sustainable economic development.

The Lebanese digital transformation draft strategy strongly relies on standards that allow technological interoperability, re-use of digital resources, data sharing and quality assurance through the government's reform plan. Setting government coherent standards for citizen-driven content and public services will help smoothen the digital transformation across the public sector. Standardisation increases efficiency, efficient connectivity and communication, maintain continuity in the digital interface of consumers and, where appropriate, ensure compliance with international standards.

The OECD Recommendation on Digital Government Strategies encourages the establishment of high-level governance and co-ordination to guarantee comprehensive collaboration and oversight of the digital government agenda (OECD, 2014[10]). An operational co-ordination structure is also needed to address implementation challenges and overcome bottlenecks. These two levels of co-ordination can be particularly helpful in maintaining the coherence, sustainability and continuity of the decisions, strategies and programmes to be adopted. The establishment of strategic co-operation processes also allows stronger surveillance, towards coherence, and gives the ability to provide decision-makers with an extensive range of projects and initiatives across sectors and levels of government. It can also allow a more straightforward evaluation of investment impacts. A co-operative environment between public stakeholders enables for better management of government operations through the return of information and data. It also allows the creation of transparency processes, which are essential for strengthening peoples' overall trust in public services and the government in general.

The institutional model foreseen by the digital transformation draft strategy of Lebanon demonstrates the country commitment to deeply strengthen cross-sector co-ordination and implementation of digital government policies. The foreseen Ministerial Committee for Digital Economy and Digital Transformation (MC4DEDT) will guarantee high-level political support and the Steering Committee for Digital Economy and Digital Transformation (SC4DEDT) will secure co-ordination across different public sector stakeholders. Additionally, the involvement of the ecosystem of stakeholders is institutionalised through the Public and Private Advisory Board (PPAB) and the co-ordinated implementation needs through the Programme Management Office (PgMO), the different Digital Transformation Units (DTU) and Project Implementation Units (PIU) across the administration.

Besides cross-sector co-ordination, sound cross-level processes and dynamics are also a critical governance variable of analysis. Encouraging powerful central government support for the governance of digital government means moving from agency-centric policies to framework solutions, concentrating on the advantages of improved policy action. A culture of co-operation can be further encouraged or fostered by organisational mechanisms that promote inter-governmental collaboration and consensus, facilitate an exchange of opinions, knowledge and information sharing among public actors on a broad-based framework of goals and priorities, and collective implementation practices.

In the case of Lebanon, there seems to exist a consensus about the excessive administrative centralisation at public administrations, knowing that such centralisation narrows the prerogatives and role of regional units and municipalities and puts on the central administration a heavy burden of duties. Municipalities depend on the orientations and resources made available by the central government. The central government and its local operatives have the prerogative of approving or rejecting any decision taken by a municipal council and consequently stop the work of municipalities. Besides, the heavy reliance on the central government for financial support places local autonomy at risk, especially in the absence of or manipulation of criteria that govern the distribution of funding from international financial institutions.

From the Taif agreements of 22 October 1989, administrative decentralisation is regularly mentioned by analysts and political leaders as a significant solution to issues such as the economic development of territories, the efficiency of public action or the fight against corruption. However, almost 30 years later, its legislative implementation has not been achieved: Parliament indeed adopted none of the numerous legislative proposals presented in the 1990s and 2000s. As part of the implementation of the structural reforms requested during CEDRE conference organised in Paris in April 2018 to support Lebanon development and reforms, the Government of Lebanon has a unique opportunity to rethink the administrative organisation scheme of its territory to best develop its economic potential and find the conditions for the maintenance of "social peace". One of the first principles of decentralisation is the presence of common interests specific to the region. As a result, shared economic interests take precedence over other interests such as the confessional political identity which seems to be one of the structuring elements of the planned division.

Considering the assessment expressed above on cross-sector and level co-ordination, three areas of improvement could help to achieve successful and efficient policy action in the case of digital government:

3. **Shared policy execution**: Although the policy oversight role of the Ministerial Committee for Digital Economy and Digital Transformation (MC4DEDT) and of the Steering Committee for Digital Economy and Digital Transformation (SC4DEDT) are critical foundations of stable and sustainable digital government development, strong policy efforts should be committed to ensuring a shared implementation of the new digital transformation draft strategy. A shared implementation approach framework promotes increasing digital government capacities across the administration and also encourages a sense of joint ownership and shared responsibility.

4. **Strengthened compliance with current rules and norms**: Most OECD member countries have significant capacity to develop and enforce rules and standards through their jurisdictions. In Lebanon, there is still big room for improvement to comply successfully with relevant digital government rules and standards. For instance, the value of data exchange across the administration should be embraced as a critical priority. This can be articulated with strengthened co-operation, assistance and capacity building across different policy areas and levels of government.

5. **Improved mobilisation of different levels of government**: Increased involvement and autonomy of local governments would favour more decentralised and sustainable digital transformation of the public sector. Mobilisation and aid across levels of government to support multilevel digital transformation agendas are essential to enabling a nation to sustain its digital development and secure that the digital transformation draft strategy is recognised as a policy for the state. The Government of Lebanon should consider enhancing strategy execution at the local stage, allowing initiatives and projects to be developed more in line with local needs, and promote the growth of local ecosystems of digital government stakeholders. Improved communication for local mobilisation, and the development of organisational areas for efficient co-operation such as regular meetings of CIOs across the entire administration could also be considered for cross-level co-ordination and co-operation.

References

AbouAssi, K. (2015), "Giving in Lebanon: Traditions and Reality in an Unstable Environment", *in* Wiepking P., Handy F. (eds.). *The Palgrave Handbook of Global Philanthropy*, https://doi.org/10.1057/978113734153_20 (accessed on 25 May 2020). [2]

European Commission (2001), *European Governance: A White Paper*, https://ec.europa.eu/commission/presscorner/detail/en/DOC_01_10 (accessed on 25 May 2020). [7]

Lebanese Arabic Institute (2020), *Administrative Divisions of Lebanon*, https://www.lebanesearabicinstitute.com/administrative-divisions-lebanon/ (accessed on 11 April 2020). [3]

OECD (2019), *The Path to Becoming a Data-Driven Public Sector*, https://doi.org/10.1787/059814a7-en. [9]

OECD (2016), *Digital Government in Chile: Strengthening the Institutional and Governance Framework*, https://dx.doi.org/10.1787/9789264258013-en. [8]

OECD (2014), *Recommendation of the Council on Digital Government Strategies*, https://legalinstruments.oecd.org/en/instruments/OECD-LEGAL-0406. [10]

OECD (forthcoming), "OECD Digital Government Project: E-Leaders Governance Handbook", *E-Leaders Task Force on Governance*. [1]

OMSAR (2019), *Lebanon Digital Transformation: Strategies to Actions (2020 – 2030), Office of the Minister of State for Administrative Reform, Republic of Lebanon, Beirut.*. [4]

Oueidat, L. (2018), *Report on National Digital Transformation Strategy of 2018*. [5]

WIPO (1990), *Constitution of Lebanon – Promulgated May 23, 1926 with its amendments,*, https://www.wipo.int/edocs/lexdocs/laws/en/lb/lb018en.pdf. [6]

Chapter 4. **Policy levers**

This chapter explores the policy levers that the Government of Lebanon can use in its governance of the public sector digital transformation. The OECD E-Leaders Governance Handbook describes "policy levers as tools that can be used by governments as a means of action in specific sectors to achieve system-wide change. Digital government policy levers are also fundamental for promoting the use of crucial enablers across the administration. To sustain sound digital government, the effective adoption of these critical enablers is one of the essential challenges faced by governments of OECD member and non-member countries. By actively promoting the adoption of the enablers through the different policy levers, governments are reinforcing the implementation capacity of their digital government policies' delivery and adoption" (OECD, forthcoming[1]).

The role of policy levers in the governance of digital government

Effective governance structures include specific scopes, functions and duties in the creation, management, execution and evaluation of digital government initiatives. Public sector organisations responsible for digital transformation provide consultative and decision-making duties. Leading institutions have at their disposal soft and hard policy levers to ensure successful execution of the agenda – such as supervision and guidance for the former, and decision-making authority and compulsory review of initiatives for the latter. A review of government structures by the OECD reveals that there is no single one-size-fits-all model. Furthermore, the implementation effectiveness of the governance system is mainly relational, dependent on the variety of factors within the general institutional framework of the region. Policy tools to support policy co-ordination, implementation, compliance and enforcement should be considered to ensure that they can be successful instruments of the digital transition of the public sector (OECD, forthcoming[1]).

The critical policy levers for the successful and sustainable governance of digital governments are a solid national digital government policy strategy and plan, a designated governing body and effective leadership and enforcement capacity. Governments are encouraged to follow the creation of a digital governance framework, the use of business cases, project management frameworks, guidelines or criteria for ICT commissioning and investment thresholds, to drive effective delivery through sectors and levels of the public sector. These are crucial artefacts in guiding policy action in work-streams that are constantly and rapidly evolving. Developing analytical tools or policy mechanisms to track new programmes or initiatives enable policy makers to co-ordinate political action and make cost-benefit analyses of the effectiveness of public investment. It is also a systematic way of ensuring the performance, efficacy and alignment of procurement processes, and of the gaps or overlaps that may emerge from agency-driven approaches (OECD, forthcoming[1]).

Based on the E-Leaders Task Force on Governance inputs and the OECD Recommendation on Digital Government Strategies (OECD, 2014[2]), the dimensions and sub-dimensions within the policy levers facet are suggested as instruments that enable better and more sustainable design and implementation of digital government policies and agendas (see Figure 4.1).

Figure 4.1. Digital government policy levers

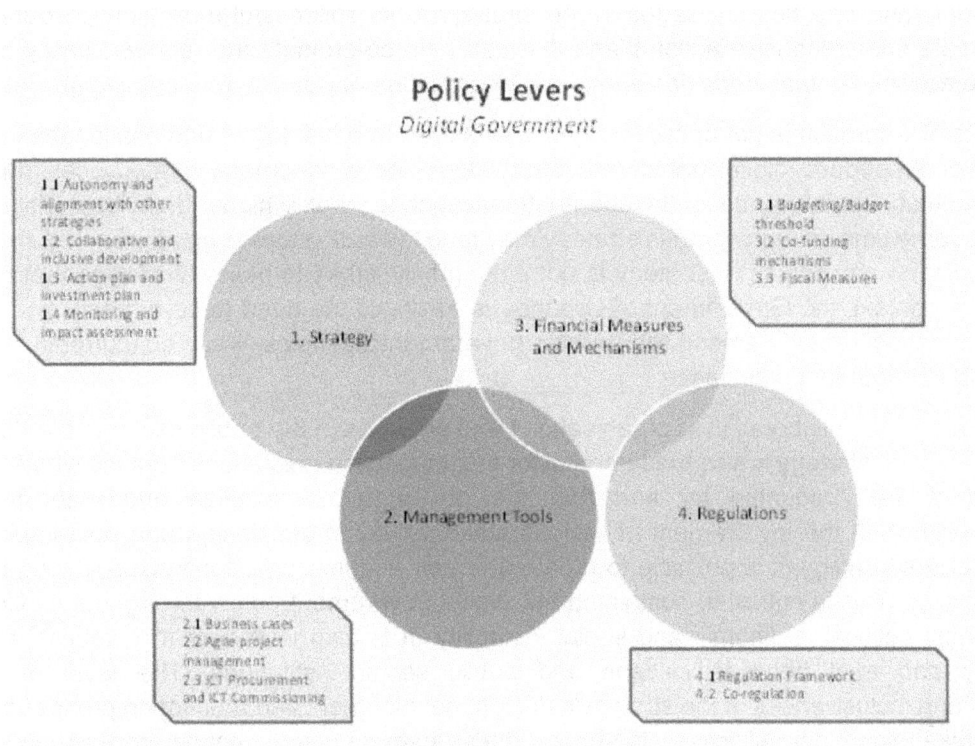

Source: (OECD, forthcoming[1]) OECD E-Leaders Governance Handbook.

The planning, execution, monitoring and evaluation of digital government policies, based on an appropriate action plan and investment plan, is key to success in driving the digital transformation of the public sector. Lebanon's willingness to use digital technologies to modernise the country's public sector and facilitate a more equitable distribution of growth results must rely heavily on its operational capacity to identify, schedule, execute and track ICT projects to ensure adequate returns on investments. Weak prioritisation and preparation of ICT programmes have led to significant delays. Furthermore, ICT project management has become highly sophisticated in terms of expenditure scale, number of partners participating, resource strategy processes, variety of technical choices and overall project management techniques involving more advanced and interdisciplinary skills. Creating these skills is a significant challenge for sub-national governments dealing with limited resources like the case of Lebanon. Despite significant benefits, due to their existence, they may turn into substantial transaction costs to maintain successful alignment and co-ordinated opportunities and actions.

The following segments will look at critical areas for capacity building to establish a digital government and data-driven public sector, namely: 1) strategy; 2) management tools; 3) financial measures and mechanisms; 4) regulations.

Dimension 1. Strategy

A digital government and governance strategy, collaborative approaches to its construction, development, implementation and monitoring are crucial to a robust and sustainable digital transformation of the public sector. Such a strategy can align goals, objectives and initiatives, and is fundamental in building consensus and contributing to the necessary cross-government co-ordination for efficient and effective implementation. The efficient, cohesive, organised, and consistent execution of these policies is one of the policy challenges currently facing OECD member and non-member states. Capacity to switch from the concept of goals and priorities envisaged in the strategy to its successful execution encourages policy makers to create comprehensive action plans that can help co-ordinate the required policy intervention and collective actions through industries and levels of government (OECD, forthcoming[1]).

A one-size-fits-all approach is not applicable because there are advantages and challenges in having an autonomous or embedded digital transformation strategy. An autonomous strategy can have greater political and institutional relevance for the country to advance towards a higher digital maturity of its public sector. At the same time, an autonomous strategy may tend towards a top-down approach in the execution and implementation process if the strategy is not thoughtfully linked to policy strategies that cover other sectors. In this context, the Government of Lebanon is aware of the need to co-ordinate and organise a digital transformation strategy among the various government agencies, while concurrently ensuring its autonomy and strength for continuance.

The co-ordination and collaboration of organisations and agencies in the public sector in the design of the digital transformation strategy is also fundamental for ensuring that expectations from the whole ecosystem of stakeholders are accounted for and that the government can align and meet their needs comprehensively. With the involvement of various stakeholders in the design and post-implementation assessment of the strategy, it is possible to create an open and inclusive consensus among both public and private actors. This is critical to sustaining the digital government policy throughout its lifecycle and despite potential political, economic and social instability. It is also important to establish a system of accountability and trust between citizens and public sector institutions. The level of openness, transparency and inclusiveness of the strategy's design, development and monitoring process will indicate how willing stakeholders are collectively to support the strategy's implementation process.

The process of implementing a good digital transformation strategy also requires governments to develop comprehensive action plans. Lebanon's action plan presents strategic objectives that accompany the digital transformation draft strategy, a brief roadmap featuring different stages to be accomplished from establishing a governance structure to forming an implementation task force and developing specific plans and teams with defined roles and responsibilities – before pre-requisite and priority programmes and solutions can be executed. There will also be monitoring and evaluation mechanisms with key performance indicators (KPIs). In such as case, the Government of Lebanon is aware of what an action plan should contain and that it should guarantee the continued development of a robust, coherent, sustainable action plan that is built on top of strong institutional models. Each programme and solution that has been highlighted as a pre-requisite and priority must be accompanied by actionable measures and achievable roadmaps. Particular attention must be paid to digital key enablers as they are the "building blocks" on which digital services can be developed and innovated quickly. In Portugal, for instance, digital key enablers such as the digital identity, the interoperability platform, the single digital gateway and public e-procurement were among the first cross-sector digital projects and they still serve as major driving forces for digital transformation of the public sector, economy and society today, while still adapting to new contexts, technologies and trends.

The plan of action should be able to show the process of implementation of the digital transformation strategy, based on proper management processes, an appropriate sharing of roles within public sector organisations and the participation of actors from the digital government community (private sector, academia and civil society). It involves a structure of the necessary policy action and public efforts across sectors and levels of government. A precise definition of duties and responsibilities is key to maintaining effective policy enforcement. Since efficient implementation also depends on dynamic contexts and changing variables, especially when the digital transformation is considered to be ongoing, agility in the planning phase can be decisive in ensuring that the action plan is permanently adapted to the contextual reality it is intended to apply. Agile project management of the action plan is expected based on effective tracking processes and periodic revisions to the steps and deadlines for execution. The ability of policy makers to be flexible in the implementation of the action plan will decide its lasting importance, preventing the obsolescence of this crucial policy mechanism.

The relation of digital government strategies with broader reform agendas is also a fundamental dimension of analysis to understand their relevance and sustainability. The capacity of governments to establish strong links and bridges between their digital government strategy and other reform agendas demonstrates their level of maturity in understanding the digital transformation underway. For sound policy development, the OECD Recommendation on Digital Government Strategies underlines that "digital government strategies need to become firmly embedded in mainstream modernisation policies" (OECD, 2014[2]). This will promote improved co-ordination and synergies but will also allow relevant stakeholder outside of government to be included and feel ownership for the outcomes of major policy reforms.

Lebanon has produced a hybrid embedded strategy in a single document the country's main goals and priorities, as the digital government priorities are part of the CEDRE agreement plans and concern broader plans (digital economy and social strategy, administrative simplification strategy). A wide variety of actors in the public administration are meant to co-operate in the preparation and execution of digital development programmes (Oueidat, 2018[3]).

Finally, it is key to further develop proper monitoring and impact assessment mechanisms, namely through KPIs. Governments need to be able to properly monitor the implementation and performance of the strategies and action plans. This will provide information and intelligence for the smarter design of new policies, and the improvement of existing ones. A sound monitoring capacity is also integral to enabling transparency through the policy design and implementation process and instilling trust in the public sector by citizens and the private sector. Furthermore, open monitoring mechanisms can help to boost accountability and commitment of the stakeholders. A robust framework for the measurement of outputs, outcomes and impacts of the digital government strategy shows the level of maturity of the public sector in adopting transparent, accountable and evidence-based policymaking approaches. Finally, the monitoring and impact assessment tools are best to be employed in the context of agile project management. It should also involve a dynamic review of the project objectives, priorities and actions in line with the changing context.

The Government of Lebanon has expressed its desire to improve the management of its performance, transparency and efficiency in the digital transformation. It has devised a comprehensive performance management programme where the public administration is to measure performance for improvement and use the measurements for performance budgeting and strategic planning. One challenge in this area is the poor access to and sharing of operational information and financial data due to the units still functioning in silos and the presence of inconsistency among them. The Access to Information Law (Number 28) was adopted in 2017 but it has not been effectively implemented until 2019, where OMSAR began developing a National Action Plan with United Nations Development Programme and the OECD. The implementation process involves consultation with civil society organisations, participation in awareness raising activities, training for public information officers and development of guides for citizens on the law. A digital government that has integrated adequate access to shared data and a culture of openness will be the first milestone, which would then open doors to the standardisation of performance data, performance evaluation, and the production of data-driven insights to improve performance over time.

Under the Organisational Performance Inspection Programme, OMSAR and the Central Inspection (CI) have developed a comprehensive set of generic and sectoral KPIs for its ministries and public agencies, under six priority key performance areas (KPAs): citizen centricity; business centricity; digital governments solutions and applications; digital infrastructure; digital transformation policies and legal framework; digital transformation ethics, norms and standards. Further to this, additional KPIs will be defined after the strategy and implementation plan are approved by the Council of Ministers. These efforts dedicated to the design and development of these robust monitoring and impact assessment programmes will ensure that the digital government strategies and action plans being implemented can lead towards the attainment of the correct outputs, outcomes and impacts.

Dimension 2. Management tools

Business case methodologies can be crucial in ensuring the success of the digital transformation of the public sector, their alignment with key priority objectives and the capacity of the public sector to take corrective measures and show strategic vision and agility needed to deliver results according to the expectations. They help prepare ICT projects and identify the necessary use of project management resources and expertise. The lack of such practices makes it difficult to formulate strong value propositions make a case to justify IT investments, and to show their beneficial results for the public administration, people and businesses, and thus secure the political commitment and public support. Agile ICT procurement approaches are important in increasing the efficiency and effectiveness of activities by the government and public sector in the face of limited resources and budgets. An evolution from an ICT procurement approach focused on the technology to an ICT commissioning culture where providers are involved earlier in the commissioning process through agile mechanisms and proper feedback loops is fundamental to deliver value and realise benefits in the digital age.

ICT investments have become highly demanding in terms of expenditure scale, stakeholder participation and technical readiness. The use of strong business cases, covered by Principle 9 of the OECD Recommendation is one of the policy processes for ICT ventures which defines the importance or gain of the initiative and clarifies the compatibility of the technology with the strategic objectives of the enterprise and the public sector more generally (OECD, 2014[2]). Clear business scenarios help to make investment decisions focused on a comprehensive cost-benefit analysis and help determine project threats early on, helping project managers to establish effective risk management plans.

Denmark, for example, has significantly improved the ICT project governance and execution through the creation of structured business cases and ICT project management frameworks, the use of which is compulsory across the government for projects with a budget of more than DKK 10 million. The Danish approach encourages tracking of the achievement of the intended gains and the achievement of the pre-established goals. Based on the objectives set by the business case, the ICT project management structure allows to monitor and assess implementation, identify deficiencies and make timely adjustments to the implementation of the project. Due to the various monitoring processes of the management cycle, these instruments are a significant source of data, helping the public sector organisation in charge to recognise performance factors and shortcomings in government ICT programmes, while continually improving the public sector's capacity to handle initiatives that are becoming more complicated. New Zealand has also implemented a "Better Business Case (BBC) Methodology" to ensure smarter investments (see Box 4.1).

Box 4.1. New Zealand's Better Business Cases (BBC) methodology

The primary objective of the BBC is to enable smart investment decisions for public value. If applied appropriately BBC can also help to: •reduce the costs of developing business cases •reduce the time it takes to develop business cases •meet recognised good practice A business case is the vehicle to demonstrate that a proposed investment is strategically aligned, represents value for money, and is achievable. A business case turns an idea (think) into a proposal (plan). It enables decision-makers to invest with confidence, knowing that they have the best information available at a point in time. It is also a reference point during the "do" phase to support delivery and used in the review phase to determine whether the benefits in the business case were realised. For significant projects, there are two key stages in the evolution of a project business case: the indicative business case and the detailed business case. For smaller and/or lower-risk investments, typically a single-stage business case (which combines the indicative and detailed business cases) is used.

Source: (The Treasury, 2020[4]) "Better Business Case (BBC)", https://treasury.govt.nz/information-and-services/state-sector-leadership/investment-management/better-business-cases-bbc.

The Government of Lebanon may benefit from the use of such policy levers at the central administration level and the creation of use cases, models and guidelines promoting their use at different levels of government. Therefore, the use of business cases can help to develop main project metrics that can be tracked. The radical integration of these indicators into the governance of ICT initiatives in the public sector at all levels will help promote a culture based on performance and outcomes in the adoption of digital governance in Lebanon. These indicators will enable project managers to make immediate changes to project execution and help the more comprehensive government recognise the main factors of project successes and failures. In fact, by gathering these details, the public sector organisation in-charge of the Digital transformation will improve its capacity to track the execution of digital government policies continually. The value of these resources can be increased if they are complemented with models and instructions on ICT project management and instruction on the use of such materials presented to its most probable consumers.

Efforts to modernise the government in Lebanon would inevitably involve the development of the digital infrastructure and services, and the accompanying financing and investments required. New digital technologies, such as cloud computing, enable organisations to access services and infrastructure on demand, track their workload, promote co-operation between public bodies and facilitate the broad adoption of specific strategic solutions for the public administration. The efficiency gains facilitated by this technological advance make it particularly cost-effective relative to the construction and maintenance of a private data centre. Such technological approaches are encouraging new ways of collaboration and sharing of resources. This has prompted several governments around the world to transfer significant portions of their computing power, data management and access to services to publicly or privately managed clouds.

Nevertheless, these same innovations raise new challenges for which existing procurement systems are unable to provide answers frequently. These include threats of technical lock-in or possible breaches of data privacy and security. A more mature digital environment that defines the need to provide Lebanon's government at all levels with easy access to digital services and infrastructure, requires new decision-making tools that can take these new variables into account. As such, new approaches to procurement would allow policy makers and decision-makers to create cost-benefit analyses and assessments that help to address such uncertainties. For instance, if Lebanon decides to heavily invest in national data centres for public institutions, the choice should be made with careful consideration of the options currently available, including cloud computing, with its advantages and disadvantages.

The OECD Recommendation on Digital Government Strategies' Principle 11 recommends that to enhance ICT procurement efficiency in favour of the digital transformation of the government sector, states will buy technology based on existing infrastructure. These frameworks should enable a co-ordinated strategy that remains flexible enough to accommodate various types of ICT procurement and public-private partnerships and deployments. Nonetheless, this depends on the existence of some resources to help strategic decisions to prevent duplication of spending. Definitions of such resources provide searchable databases or archives containing all current ICT contracts and properties, or statistics on the past performance of ICT companies. Nevertheless, the Lebanese bodies currently lack similar tools. The several digital government stakeholders interviewed during the OECD fact-finding mission to Beirut in June 2019 recognised other weaknesses such as lacking budgets for sustainability and recurring costs, and post-release updates, further developments, maintenance and enhancements for efficient procurement and funding. To counter this, the Government of Lebanon could prioritise the development of an appropriate legal and policy approach for ICT investments. It should also adopt procurement laws that are conducive to public e-procurement across its public sector and economy.

Dimension 3. Financial measures and mechanisms

Economic incentives are crucial to promote ICT projects and initiatives and ensure an effective digital transformation of the public sector. These financial measures and mechanisms include grants, subsidies, immediate and indirect financing and public-private partnerships that the government can count on. Investment plans can facilitate the successful execution of the draft digital government strategy through the proper identification and distribution of financial resources to the public sector agencies involved. Investment plans are also essential tools for cost-benefit analysis, helping policy makers and other partners to track better investments and the interest that they will achieve. The capacities and capabilities necessary for a sound digital government policy involve strong budgeting capacities, co-funding mechanisms and fiscal measures to support ICT procurement and commissioning.

A digital transformation strategy presents a useful means for planning and managing financing and investments in deploying digital technology across the government and the public sector. The directions set by the strategy will condition the types of projects that would be funded and prioritised. A certain degree of allowance is needful in this context for efficient and flexible resource allocation according to changing needs and supply of ICTs. When it comes to the project selection criteria and monitoring, the Government of Lebanon has the requirement for the main contracting authority, the beneficiary and the contractor to demonstrate the ability to commit human and financial resources during and post-project implementation. Financial audits are to be conducted by the Digital Transformation Steering Committee (DEDTSC) to ensure that projects are in line with budgets. A key performance sub-area under digital transformation ethics, norms and standards (S-KPA 6.4) covers the establishment of financial management and electronic reporting procedures for digital transformation projects. This is a positive measure in the provision of ICT project investment guidelines and norms to steer change. The Government of Lebanon should consider setting more comprehensive targets and guidelines detailing financial measures and mechanisms to adequately address various mandates and steps of the digital transformation draft strategy and provide the public sector innovators with the right incentives and resources. In the consideration of ICT projects, the digitalisation of non-ICT sectors also plays an important role and should not be neglected, as it has become increasingly clear that digitalisation can generate a competitive advantage across all sectors.

Further areas for development include budgeting, budget thresholds, co-funding mechanisms and fiscal measures. Under the Government of Lebanon's implementation roadmap, specific implementation plans will be undertaken as the third stage after the establishment of the governance structure and the formation of the implementation task force. The project implementation plan will include operating budgets, funding and risk management to ensure the sustainability of the operations. OMSAR already recognises that project planning and budget preparation are the most crucial steps for the success of the digital transformation. It highlights that sustainability funding needs to account for capital investment in ICTs, operational running costs, preventive maintenance and periodic service costs, and human resources and skills development costs. It also underlines that is key for the budget to have planned receipts and expenditures.

The capacity to influence budgetary priorities in a country and how financial resources are distributed in the public sector is important in determining the success of policy implementation. Political influence, the capacity of aligning specific objectives with broader national policy agenda and technical expertise are also fundamental determinants of a successful policy process. OMSAR and the Lebanese Digital Agency should build on such a cross-cutting role that can reinforce the institutional influence, mandate and stakeholder support in the ecosystem for a successful digital transformation of the public sector.

Budget thresholds serve as another important policy lever for pre-evaluation of investments in digital technologies, greater alignment across the administration, better coherence and sustainability of the investments made, and avoiding gaps and overlap in the investments. This mechanism will encourage a systems-thinking approach that promotes consistent public expenses across the administration, stimulate co-operation and build synergies across different bodies of the government. This is especially crucial for Lebanon, which needs to have streamlined, efficient and effective governance structures and processes that serve as a strong foundation for a data-driven, user-centric and agile system – one that responds to policy changes and continual adaptations despite uncertain contextual factors. In addition, budget thresholds also encourage transparency and accountability of investments and financial efforts, to the private sector, civil society and citizens.

On the one hand, oversight and control mechanisms like business cases, budget and budget thresholds enforce policy coherence. On the other hand, fiscal measures and financial incentives like co-funding are important in activating institutional wills, strengthening commitments and securing alignment positively. Co-funding mechanisms help to encourage participation, engagement and proactiveness in creating solutions – thereby having spill-over effects in innovation and entrepreneurship in both public and private sectors. Co-funding needs to be aligned strongly with existing digital government mechanisms and policies such that the initiatives and projects rolled out will fully benefit from financial support.

The aforementioned financial measures and mechanisms are critical success factors for effective, coherent and sustainable implementation in Lebanon. Building on the strong efforts and commitments underway to enhance the digital transformation of the public sector, the Lebanese government should prioritise the development of these policy levers in the new digital government framework for sound policy implementation capacity.

Dimension 4. Regulations

Laws and regulations have always been a critical component in public policy and can play a significant role in transforming markets, changing behaviour and removing barriers that impede progress. They need to be in place for digital change to be institutionalised and secured in the government and the public sector – a crucial part of ensuring new policies and processes are implemented and under compliance. Following Principle 12 of the OECD Recommendation on Digital Government Strategies, policy makers are required to "ensure that general and sector-specific legal and regulatory frameworks allow digital opportunities digital opportunities to be seized" namely by "reviewing them as appropriate".

Because of the cross-cutting effect of digital transition in markets, communities and governments, multiple laws and regulations need to be built from the outset or better revised to allow and facilitate digital reform.

The diversity of trends and complexity of digital systems requires a correspondingly sophisticated legal and regulatory digital framework. Furthermore, the approach and model for these frameworks are dependent on individual legal and regulatory environments and institutional cultures.

A few legal and regulatory building blocks should nonetheless still be present for a sound institutionalisation of the digital transformation (see Figure 4.2). Some domains to be highlighted in line with Lebanon's digital areas of development are the reinforcement of digital rights of citizens and businesses, the protection of personal data and cyber security.

Figure 4.2. Legal and regulatory framework for institutionalising the digital transformation

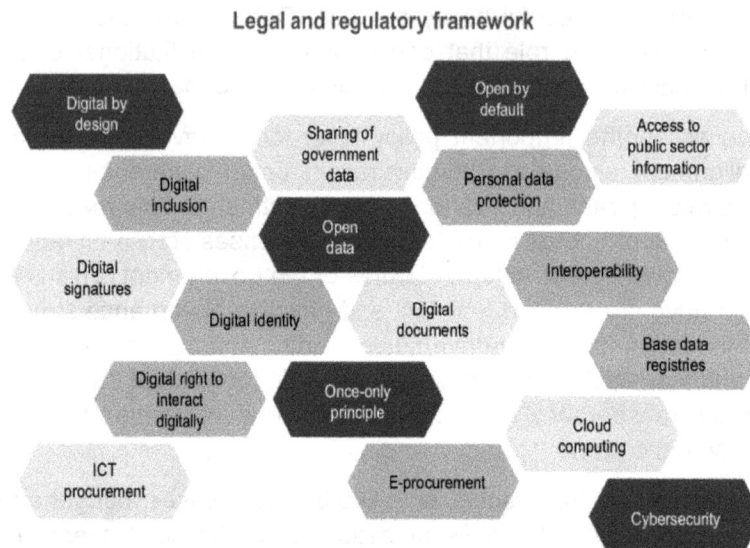

Legal and regulatory framework

Source: (OECD, 2019[5]), Digital Government Review of Panama: Enhancing the Digital Transformation of the Public Sector, https://doi.org/10.1787/615a4180-en.

Lebanon's digital transition will involve reviews and modifications of the legal frameworks as well as new legislations, decisions and decrees. The Government of Lebanon has identified overregulation and excessive bureaucracy at one end and low-enforcement and corruption as the other challenges. To overcome this, the government will need to design purposeful regulation targeting digital technologies that improve agility, performance, innovation, efficiency, transparency and accountability. Overregulation of administrative procedures should also be reduced using ICT and digital technologies, by ridding of paperwork and streamlining processes. Another stage in this dimension that could pose a challenge in Lebanon are the bureaucratic and political hurdles of the design and endorsement of laws and regulations. To change this, the government needs to encourage a significant change in mindset and culture to make civil servants responsible and accountable through programmes and incentives. At the same time, as mentioned above (in Chapter 2 on Contextual Factors), beyond the need of an updated legal and regulatory framework, enhancing the digital transformation of the public sector is not a static process, requiring an agile, collaborative and experimental culture across the administration that can go beyond legalistic approaches.

Adopting more participatory approaches, to involving the private sector and civil society in the design of regulations and rules covering the aforementioned digital areas, especially those that concern citizens and businesses directly, is another approach to ensure that laws are institutionalised effectively. Frequent consultation and communication, in line with the OECD Recommendation of the Council on Open Government, will increase the public sector openness and bring it closer to other stakeholders and allow faster recognition and adoption of regulations materially. OMSAR has identified civic engagement as a key pillar for the digital transformation of Lebanon. It recognises the importance of identifying all issues and problems from reliable stakeholders. It will also be important to secure alignment with the goals and objectives of the government's digital transformation draft strategy. In the governance of its digital transformation draft strategy that eventually makes it to new digital government policies, it is most critical for the Government of Lebanon to take an active and inclusive approach to understand its contextual factors, improving its institutional models and designing targeted and important policy levers engaging the whole ecosystem of stakeholders.

References

OECD (2019), "Digital Government Review of Panama: Enhancing the Digital Transformation of the Public Sector", *OECD Digital Government Studies*, https://doi.org/10.1787/615a4180-en. [5]

OECD (2014), *Recommendation of the Council on Digital Government Strategies*, https://legalinstruments.oecd.org/en/instruments/OECD-LEGAL-0406. [2]

OECD (forthcoming), "OECD Digital Government Project: E-Leaders Governance Handbook", *E-Leaders Task Force on Governance*. [1]

Oueidat, L. (2018), *Report on National Digital Transformation Strategy of 2018*. [3]

The Treasury (2020), *Better Business Case (BBC) Information and services: State sector leadership: Investment management system*, https://treasury.govt.nz/information-and-services/state-sector-leadership/investment-management/better-business-cases-bbc. [4]